How to JUMP-START Your (Next) CAREER

I0041151

How to JUMP-START Your (Next) CAREER

DALE CARNEGIE

MANJUL
Manjul Publishing House

First published in India by

Manjul Publishing House
- C-16, Sector 3, Noida, Uttar Pradesh 201301 – India
  Website: www.manjulindia.com
Registered Office:
- 10, Nishat Colony, Bhopal 462 003 - India

The Success Series:
How to Jump-Start Your (Next) Career by *Dale Carnegie*

This edition first published in India in 2018

Copyright © Dale Carnegie & Associates
Rights licensed exclusively by JMW Group Inc.
jmwgroup@jmwgroup.net

ISBN 978-93-87383-29-6

Cover Design by Trinankur Banerjee

This edition is authorised for sale in the Indian Subcontinant only.

Printed and bound in India by Repro India Ltd.

CONTENTS

Preface

For most of us, second to our family, the most important part of our lives is the work we do. Whether we work as an assembler on a production line, a clerk in an office, a sales rep in the field, a physician, the owner of a small business, an engineer or a college professor, we spend more time in our occupation than in most other segments of our lives.

Some of us have selected our careers only after carefully learning much about our line of work, some of us have gone through extensive education or training to qualify for our positions, still others fell into our careers by fortuity. Some of us love the work we've chosen, some hate it, others find it tolerable but are not truly happy in it.

Many of us look at our current position as a rung on the career ladder—each rung moving us into a higher position. We work hard and make every effort to acquire the skills and knowledge to warrant advancement. Yet there are some of us who are perfectly content with the job we have and make no effort to advance. Although this book is written for men and women in the former category, there is no shame in being satisfied to remain in one's current position until retirement.

In some jobs, the advancement opportunities would serve to eliminate what it is we love about our work. Marcy was a teacher of social studies in the New York City public schools. In 2010, she received the award as the best teacher in the entire city high school system. She was encouraged to apply for an assistant principal's job, but refused. Marcy said, "My forte and my joy is working with the students. I have no desire to move into administration." Marcy never regretted her decision and continues enjoying teaching and dealing directly with her students on a day-to-day basis.

Some of us may seek advancement, but when we move to a management position, we are not happy. Our real love is working in our speciality and we miss that when promoted. When Charles Kettering, inventor of the electric ignition system and dozens of other products, became a Vice President of General Motors, he found no satisfaction in management and requested reassignment to a position where he could concentrate on his creative abilities.

If we are, however, one of those people who truly wish to advance in our careers, we should investigate what types of positions we will engage in as we climb that ladder. In the world of business, there are two roads we may take in advancing in our careers. One is the management road in which we will oversee people and processes. The other is the staff road in which we may not have any supervisory responsibility, but we will deal with many administrative matters.

In the first part of this book, we will discuss the preparation one must take to qualify for advancement. In order to succeed in either supervisory or administrative management, we must create a professional demeanor that is, an image that we project to our bosses, our subordinates, and our colleagues. In addition, we must develop our own personal brand—how we differ from (and are superior to) other employees who may compete with us for advancement.

This overview will be followed by a detailed discussion of how we can acquire some of the most important facets of a management position:

- Our ability in basic management processes:
  Planning, delegating, and time management
- Enhancing our people management skills:
  Knowing and motivating our staff
- Perfecting our public speaking skills:
  Preparing and making effective oral presentations
- Building up our writing skills:
  Professional letters, memos, reports, and email messages

First, we will discuss the steps to be taken to grow our career. These steps will include how we can:

- Advance within our current organization:
  Analyze opportunities

  Become visible

  Transfer to a different position

  Promotion
- Sources for seeking a new job:
  Employment agencies

Executive recruiters

Employment counselors

Networking

➤ Tools for job search:
Write and use résumés

Sell ourselves at an interview

➤ Change careers in midstream:
Make a decision

Choose a new career

Advancing in our career can be a rewarding and exciting experience. Not only do we gain financially, but we also increase our status in the organization and the community. Most importantly, our own job satisfaction is enhanced. Career advancement is not an easy task, but if we truly desire to move ahead in the field that we have chosen as well as are prepared to do the work, it is well worthwhile.

Arthur R. Pell, Ph.D.
Editor

1

CREATE A PROFESSIONAL DEMEANOR

It matters not how strait the gate,
How charged with punishments the scroll,
I am the master of my fate:
I am the captain of my soul.

William E. Henley

To paraphrase Shakespeare, some people are born to succeed, some achieve success, and some have success thrust upon them. Most of us are neither born to succeed nor have it thrust upon us. We must achieve it by good planning, hard work, and most importantly, commit ourselves to become successful in our careers. We cannot depend on others to achieve, for us. We must do it for ourselves. We must take control of our careers from its early stages, and never lose that control.

The first step on the road to success is creating a personal image that projects our commitment to achievement in our careers. Our personal image is the message we send, and the message that others receive about us. It is reflected in the signals we send to others in our words and in our actions. It is how we want to stand out from the crowd and have people remember us. We want to be known as problem solvers, outstanding team members, and diplomatic agents. We want to be perceived as polished, professional, and friendly. This image cannot be faked. It must be genuine and authentic.

Build Self-Confidence

A key ingredient to develop and maintain a strong personal image is self-confidence. Some elements of self-confidence include:

Self-Acceptance

Self-acceptance comes from our ability to accept ourselves as human beings while focusing on our positive qualities, our strengths and traits—that make us who we are. When our focus is on these areas, both confidence and self-esteem are positively influenced. It is all too common for people to focus on their weaknesses instead of their strengths. Doing this does more damage than good. We must focus on our positive qualities.

Formulate and stamp indelibly on your mind a mental picture of yourself as succeeding. Hold this picture tenaciously. Never permit it to fade. Your mind will seek to develop the picture ... Do not build up obstacles in your imagination.

Norman Vincent Peale

Self-Respect

The key to developing self-respect is to focus on our past successes and achievements and to respect ourselves for the good we have done. It is far easier to dwell on failures. Others are only too eager to point them out to us. Our perspective changes and our confidence builds when we spend time contemplating our successes.

A valuable exercise to perform is to create a "Success Inventory." This is a list of successes and accomplishments that we have had throughout our lives. At first it may be difficult to build a list, but with persistence we can keep adding to our list and building our confidence. Begin with a file folder, and start putting positive symbols and records of one's successes in it today. These may include letters from teachers commending our schoolwork, memos from employers about contributions made in jobs, emails from customers or clients thanking for good service, letters of thanks from non-profit organizations where one has contributed time and effort and similar documents. In addition, create a log in which you can enter your accomplishments and other factors of which you are particularly proud. When you feel blue or inadequate about a current situation, you can read this file and remind yourself that you succeeded before and you can do it again.

Self-Talk

All of us engage in "self-talk" like the things that we repeat to ourselves about ourselves. When we add the above items together, we create, positive self-talk backed up by evidence, an argument that would hold up under scrutiny. The stronger and more compelling the evidence, the more believable and powerful is the message. This positive self-talk is a tool to take back control of the only thing we should have ultimate control over—our thinking.

Risk Taking

We can also build our self-confidence by our readiness to take risks. We can look at new experiences as opportunities to learn rather than occasions to win or lose. Doing so opens us up to new possibilities and can increase our sense of self-esteem. Not doing so inhibits personal growth and reinforces whatever belief we may have about a new possibility being an opportunity for failure.

First Impressions

First impressions are the most lasting. Since humans are very visual beings, more than half the impression we make is based on what people see.

Appearance

People do judge a book by its cover. The impression we make is more than likely to be influenced by how we look. This does not mean that we have to be an Adonis or Venus to impress others. Though, we should be neat, well groomed, and dressed appropriately.

Appearance counts whether we are meeting executives who can determine our future in our own company for the first time or going to an interview for a new job. How we look can hurt or enhance our prospects. Attire, hairstyle, neatness, and posture have a major impact on that first impression.

Here are some of the ways by which we can ensure that we make a good impression even before that first handshake:

Choose conservative clothing.– A simple rule to follow is that it is usually best to be conservative in your choices about how you dress. Unusual clothes that draw attention to the clothes and not to the wearer should be avoided. Make sure that your attire is up-to-date. Never forget that well-groomed hair, shined shoes, proper use of makeup, and other easily seen indicators of good grooming are noted (consciously or subconsciously) by others immediately upon meeting someone.

Avoid a slovenly appearance.– Dirty fingernails, stained armpits, frayed cuffs, messy hair, unkempt beards and scuffed shoes broadcast carelessness and poor judgment.

Dress for business.– A recent college grad wore backless sandals when she interviewed last spring for a job as a hospital-laboratory research assistant. Her would-be supervisor rejected her, and when asked why by the person who referred the applicant, the supervisor commented that she feared the applicant wouldn't take her work seriously enough, citing her informal flip-flops.

Critique yourself.– A critical self-assessment can correct or prevent gaffes. We should scrutinize our appearance in front of a mirror before meeting with new people. We should also ask other people to critique our appearance. Many are eager to advise us on how to improve our appearance and dress appropriately.

Note how successful people in the organization dress.– Appropriate clothing and hairstyles vary with the type of work and industry.

For example, men and women in the fashion industry must be keenly aware of the latest fashions trends and incorporate them in their style. People working in the entertainment industry are more likely to dress casually and have contemporary hairstyles. For example, a graphic designer coming to a meeting dressed in sportswear will not be subjected to raise eyebrows, but if a banker dressed casually for a business meeting, it would be considered inappropriate.

Be Approachable

When we enter a room full of executives, clients or associates, each person intuitively asks himself whether he perceives us as approachable. If the answer is yes, the conversations in which we engage will be initiated with ease and comfort. We make new friends. We create new contacts. However, if the answer is no, there won't be any meaningful conversations. As a result, we will miss opportunities to create connections and build our network.

Pretend that every single person we meet has a sign around his or her neck that says, 'Make me feel important.' Not only will we succeed in sales, we will succeed in life.

Mary Kay Ash,
Founder of Mary Kay Cosmetics

First Impression on the Telephone

Often our first contact with another person is on the telephone. It could be a client, a prospective employer, an applicant for a position in a department or team, or a member of a government agency. The image we project in that phone call can affect the way we or the company we represent is perceived by the other person.

Jennifer was upset. The washing machine she had purchased only the month before had broken down. She called the store and asked for the manager. After six rings, the call was answered: "Jones Appliances, please hold." She waited and waited for what felt like an eternity. Just as Jennifer was about to hang up and dial again, the operator finally came back on the line:

"Jones Appliances, can I help you?"

"May I please speak to the manager?"

"What for?"

"I bought a washer last month and it broke down."

'You don't want the manager, I'll connect you with service.'

After another long wait, the service representative finally responded. Halfway through Jennifer's explanation, he interrupted her, "Sorry, we can't help you. You will have to go to the manufacturer. You'll find the address on your warranty."

and without waiting for a response, hung up. It's unlikely that Jennifer will ever buy anything from that store again.

To make a good impression on callers, answer the telephone promptly. If you work in a customer service position, and you know that the person will have to wait for any length of time, program the telephone to advise the caller that you are still talking, and give the caller the option of either continuing to wait or request a return call.

When you speak with the caller, let him or her talk until the complaint or message is fully explained. If you cannot help, give as much information as you can to enable the person to obtain the help needed. Before ending a call, ask if the caller has all the information needed or what else you can do to satisfy the person's problem. Don't forget to say "thank you" before hanging up.

Our Correspondence Also Creates First Impressions

When Warren attended a time-management seminar, he was told that the time spent on writing business letters could be shortened significantly if the writer would just jot down the response on the bottom of the letter received and mail it back to the person who sent it. Warren put this idea into practice immediately. It certainly did save time, but in doing this, the image of his company suffered. In following up a sales lead that he had answered in this matter, he learned that the prospect decided not to do business with Warren's company because he considered that their response to his inquiry was "unprofessional."

Our correspondence represents us to the public. The

letterhead should be designed to represent the image we wish to present. Spelling and typographical errors can be interpreted as indicators of a careless or inefficient operation. Intelligent readers readily detect a poor choice of words or incorrect grammar. Reread correspondence before mailing it, and make sure all letters are error-free. Don't depend on your computer's spell-check feature. It will not pick up words used improperly (for example, if you type 'of' instead of 'or.') Always proofread the letter before signing and sending it. Your letter is a permanent record of the content and style of your writing.

A poor first impression is hard to overcome. If a negative or undesirable impression is made on that first contact, it may permeate all relations with that party for years to come. It takes a little thought and effort to establish the basis for making good impressions, but it is well worth it.

In today's high-tech environment, our first contact with someone is often through email, a social networking site, or our company's or our personal website. We will discuss more about using technology to our advantage in our careers in the coming Chapters.

Personal Branding Statement

When we meet someone new, one of the first things most people ask is, "What do you do?" This is a chance for us to use our "Personal Branding Statement."

Our personal branding statement sets forth our individual skills and strengths, combines them with our interests, and identifies our unique promise of value to our listeners, whether they are clients, employees, colleagues, potential employers, or other important contacts. In order to prepare your personal branding statement, ask yourself the following questions:

> What qualities or characteristics do you have that cause to stand out from others in your field?
> What would your colleagues or clients say is your greatest strength?
> What do you do that adds or brings remarkable, measurable, distinctive value to other people and organizations?

> *Regardless of age, regardless of position, regardless of the business we happen to be in, all of us need to understand the importance of branding. We are CEOs of our own companies. To be in business today, our most important job is to be head marketer for the brand called "You."*

> Tom Peters

Relationship-Building Links

The purpose of conversational small talk is to break the ice and build a rapport. Without rapport, there is no foundation to develop a relationship. Set a goal to spend 80 percent of your time listening and 20 percent talking. As Dale Carnegie wrote, "Become genuinely interested in the other person. Be a good listener and encourage others to talk about themselves."

The following items are tips for successfully engaging in discourse with a new business associate.

Handshake

When introduced, it is appropriate to shake hands. A firm, but not bone-crushing handshake makes a good impression.

Smile. Look directly at the other person. Repeat his or her name, and take a sincere interest in what he or she is saying.

Make Positive Observations

Ask questions about the event or the surroundings. "Wasn't the speaker terrific?" "How do you think the meeting went today?"

Find a Common Denominator

Ask "What brought you here?" Often the other person attends the event for the same reason we do.

Inquire About Business

If we don't know what business the individual is engaged in, we might ask him or her. Show genuine interest and ask open-ended questions about some of the business, which is of particular interest to both of you.

Introduce Yourself

After a bit of small talk, move smoothly into telling the other person about who you are. Here's where you can use your personal branding statement and the "self-commercial."

Exchange Cards

When concluding the conversation, exchange business cards and, if appropriate, invite the person to become linked in to your online business network.

Note that your business card can be part of your personal brand. Even when using traditional business-card formats, you can add a personal touch and be memorable. However, unless you are in advertising or a related field, avoid gimmicky business cards.

When you give a business card:

> Be prepared. Have a clean supply of business cards easily accessible.
> Present the card in a manner that demonstrates it is worth something.
> Add personal details such as private number, nickname, etc.
> Present it so that it is facing up and toward the other person.

When you are given a business card:

> Stop and read the card.
> Notice the person's title and comment on it.
> Comment on the design if it is unique or creative in any way.
> Ask a question that shows your interest.
> Check to see if there is a mobile number—if not, get it.
> Check to see if there is an email address—if not, get it.
> Write the date and location and a brief note of the meeting on the back.
> Enter the information into your contact-management system.
> Follow up and send information to link the person to your network.

Make a Positive Exit

To end a conversation graciously, simply say, "It was a pleasure meeting you, (say his or her name); perhaps we could meet again in the near future," or, "It was great to meet you, (name); you will hear from me tomorrow with the link to my online business network."

Maintaining Good Relationships

Making a good first impression is only the first step in creating for yourself the professional demeanor that will determine how you are perceived by others. You must constantly be attentive when it comes to how you look, act, and interrelate with everybody with whom you are in contact. In addition, you must be able to observe and understand what others are projecting in their relations with us.

Here are some guidelines to help you make and keep a professional image.

Seven Constructive Behaviors That Propel Us Forward

1. Be trustworthy and keep confidences. Understand when it is and when it is not appropriate to share conversations and management strategies.
2. Develop an "open door" policy. Give others your complete attention when they speak and encourage them to express their concerns, interests, and the barriers preventing them from being successful. Give encouragement and praise often.
3. Always display good manners, listening skills, appropriate language, and congruency between words and actions.
4. Build positive customer and supplier relations.
5. Be confident, energetic, and a self-starter. Anticipate challenges and options to overcome them. We hear people referred to as "high maintenance" or "low maintenance." We want others to see us in the latter category, as someone who takes charge appropriately and doesn't create problems without exceptional cause.

6. Run efficient and focused meetings and provide detailed notes to all involved.

7. Be reliable, consistent and accountable.

Seven Destructive Behaviors That Hold Us Back

1. Failure to keep a confidence with colleagues, peers, and direct reports.

2. Clock-watching, taking excessive and inappropriate breaks, and leaving urgent tasks unfinished and messages unanswered.

3. Failure to offer your point of view to senior management before a decision has been made.

4. Inappropriate dress, language, and insensitivity to diversity issues.

5. Failure to participate in discussions with senior management and with staff.

6. Inability to immediately bounce back and gain composure after a frustrating or difficult time.

Reading the Nonverbal Clues of Others

All of us convey information with more than the words we use. What we say is often modified by the way we use our body. Our facial expressions, our gestures, and the way we sit or stand all convey meaning. Wouldn't it be great if we could buy a dictionary of body language so that we could look up what each gesture or expression means? Then we could interpret what everybody is really saying.

Some people have tried to write such "dictionaries," listing a variety of different "signals" and identifying their meaning. For example, the other person strokes his chin. What can this mean? "Ha! I know. He's pondering about the situation." Indeed, he may very well be thinking it over, but it might also mean that he didn't shave this morning and his chin itches.

The person across from us is sitting with her arms folded in front of her. Some "experts" interpret this to mean that she is holding herself in, blocking us out, rejecting us. Nonsense! Look at a roomful of people in a class, a lecture, or a theatrical performance. Note that a good number of these people are sitting with arms crossed. Does that mean that they are rejecting the instructor or actors? Of course not. It's a comfortable way to sit, and if we are cold, it keeps us warm. On the other hand, if in the middle of a conversation, the other party should suddenly cross her arms, it might mean that at that point she is disagreeing with us.

There is No Universal Body Language

Although there is no one body language subject to one interpretation, this does not mean that one cannot read body language. Each one of us has his or her own way of expressing ideas and feelings. Why should this be? Body language is largely an acquired trait. We tend to imitate other people, and our body language is usually acquired through our parents. Often it is closely tied in with our ethnic background. For example, two boys are born in Detroit, Michigan, but their parents immigrated to the United States from two different countries. One family came from a country where the usual way to express oneself was with gesticulation. One could not speak the language without using one's hands. The other family came from a country where nobody gesticulated except when highly emotional. The two boys met for the first time in high school. The first boy was discussing a situation in his usual way—his hands moving wildly. The second boy thought, "My goodness, he's excited about this." Then he responded in his usual quiet way, and the first boy thought, "He's not even interested."

The following story demonstrates how cultural differences affect the way we use non-verbal communication. Following the theft of money from a high school cafeteria in New York City, the principal interviewed all of the students who had access to the cash register. After the interviews, he determined that the thief was a Latin American girl and he suspended her. A social worker visited the principal about this case and asked why he felt she was the thief. He responded, "All the other students looked me straight in the eye and said that they didn't do it. This girl wouldn't look me in the eye. She looked down at her toes throughout the interview. She's obviously guilty." The social worker informed him that a well-bred Latin American girl is taught never to look straight into the face of such an exalted personage as a principal, but to look demurely to the ground when talking to him. The girl's behavior was a product of her cultural upbringing and was misinterpreted by the principal.

Similarly, body language patterns may be determined by family habits. When anybody speaks to a member of Nicole's family, he or she will be rewarded with frequent nods of the head. Most of us would interpret this to mean that the person nodding is agreeing with us. But as Nicole pointed out when questioned about this, all it meant was that he or she acknowledged hearing what was being said.

Study Each Person's Use of Nonverbal Clues

If body language is an important aspect of communication, is there any way that we can learn to read it? There is no 100 percent accurate approach to reading body language, but we can learn to obtain a reasonably good interpretation of a person's nonverbal actions and reactions by getting to know him or her. When we deal with the same people over and over again, by careful observation we can learn to read each individual's body language. We note that when Claudia agrees with us, she tends to lean forward, and when Paul agrees, he tilts his head to the right. We observe that Nicole nods no matter what we say, but when she is not sure of something, she has a puzzled look on her face even though she is nodding.

By making careful mental notes about all the people we communicate with, we will be able to understand their nonverbal clues and interpret them properly. After a while, we may note that some gestures or expressions are more common among the people we communicate with than others. From these we may make some generalizations when dealing with new people, but we must be careful not to put too much credence in generalized interpretations. It's best to have a good deal of experience with someone before we make assumptions about what a person's body language conveys.

When the body language seems to contradict or skew the meaning of the words being spoken, or we are not sure what the signal being sent really means, ask a question. Get the person to communicate verbally. By asking the right questions, we can overcome the doubts that the nonverbal actions create and we will be able to deal with them.

Lastly, we should make a point of being aware of our own body language. Moderation is the rule.

Listening Skills

For any interaction between two people to be productive, it is essential that both participants listen to each other. We must give full attention to the other person, but we must also be aware of whether that person is truly listening to us or not. Here are some of the most frequent listening problems. First, ask yourself if you fit into one or more of these categories and if so, take the recommended tips to correct it. Second, try to determine if the other person fits in this category and follow the tips so that he or she will really listen to what you are saying.

Be a good listener. Your ears will never get you in trouble.

Frank Tyger,
Editorial Commentator

Seven Types of Listeners

There are many kinds of listeners. Here is one way listeners have been characterized. As we read this list, determine if we or the person with whom we are communicating fits in some category.

1. *The "Preoccupieds."*– These people come across as rushed and are constantly looking around or doing something else. They cannot sit still and listen. *Tip:* if you are a preoccupied listener, you should make a point to set aside what you are

doing when someone is speaking to you. *Tip:* if you are dealing with a preoccupied listener, you might ask, "Is this a good time?" or say, "I need your undivided attention for just a moment." Begin with a statement that will get the person's attention, be brief, and get to the bottom line quickly because his or her attention span is short.

2. *The "Out-to-Lunchers."*– "Out-to-lunchers" are physically present, but mentally they are not. We can tell this by the blank look on their faces. They are either daydreaming or thinking about everything and anything except what we are saying. *Tip:* if you are an "out-to-lunchers," be alert, maintain eye contact, lean forward, and show interest by asking questions. *Tip:* if you are dealing with "out-to-lunchers," you can check in every now and again and ask if they understood what you were saying. As with the "preoccupied," begin with a statement that will catch their attention, be concise and to the point because their attention span is short.

3. *The "Interrupters."*– "Interrupters" are ready to chime in at any given time. They are perched and ready for a break to complete our sentences for us. They are not listening to you but are instead focused on what they want to say. *Tip:* if you are an "interrupters," you might make a point of apologizing every time you catch yourself interrupting. This will make you more conscious of it. *Tip:* if you are speaking with "interrupters," stop immediately when they chime in and let them talk, or they will never listen to you. When they are done, you might say, "As I was saying before. . ." to bring their interruption to their attention and get back to what you had been saying.

4. *The "Whatevers."*– "Whatevers" remain aloof and show little emotion when listening. They give the impression that they couldn't care less what you are talking about. *Tip:* if you are one of those "whatevers," concentrate on the full message, not just the verbal message. Make a point to listen with your eyes, ears, and heart. *Tip:* if you are dealing with "whatevers," dramatize your ideas and ask them questions to involve them in the conversation.

5. *The "Combatives."*– "Combatives" are armed and ready for war. They enjoy disagreeing and blaming others. *Tip:* if you are a "combative" listener, you must make an effort to put yourself in the speaker's shoes and understand, accept, and find merit in his or her point of view. *Tip:* to deal with combative listeners, when they disagree or blame someone, look forward instead of back. Talk about what can be done differently next time.

6. *The "Analysts."*– "Analysts" are constantly in the role of counselor or therapist and are ready to provide answers even when you have not asked for their input. They think they are great listeners and love to help. They are constantly in an analytical frame of mind and in "fix-it mode." *Tip:* if you are an "analyst," you should learn to relax and understand that not everyone is looking for an answer, solution, or advice. Some people just like bouncing ideas off others to see the answers more clearly themselves. *Tip:* if you are dealing with "analysts," you might begin by saying, "I just need to get something off my chest. I'm not looking for any advice."

7. *The "Engagers."*– "Engagers" are consciously aware listeners.

They listen with their eyes, ears, and hearts, and try to put themselves in the speaker's shoes. This is listening at the highest level. Their listening skills encourage one to continue talking and give one the opportunity to discover solutions and let the ideas unfold. We should all aim to be engaged listeners.

Listening Principles

To enhance our listening skills:

1. Maintain eye contact with the person who is talking.
2. Be sensitive to what is not being said.
3. Observe body language for incongruent messages.
4. Practice patience; speak only after the other person is finished.
5. Do not interrupt, finish the speaker's sentence, or change the subject.
6. Listen to learn; pretend there will be a quiz at the end of the conversation.
7. Clarify any uncertainties after the person is done speaking.
8. Make sure you understood what was said by paraphrasing what you heard.
9. Don't jump to conclusions or make assumptions.
10. Practice pure listening; remove all distractions.
11. When speaking, try to see things from the listeners' perspective.

   We have two ears and one mouth so that we can listen twice as much as we speak.

   Epictetus

Giving and Receiving Constructive Feedback

One type of communication that is challenging for many of us is giving and receiving criticism. Because criticism, in and of itself, is not particularly useful. One should focus on constructive feedback, which is practical information designed to help someone provide better service, or improve his or her performance. It is a two way process. We give instructions, opinions, ideas or criticism to another person; or the other person gives us similar feedback. How can we assure that we are getting what that person is saying or vice versa? Here are some tips on effectively giving and graciously receiving constructive feedback:

Giving Constructive Feedback

1. Get all the facts.
2. Address the situation promptly and privately.
3. Focus on the act or behavior, not the person.
4. Give the person a genuine compliment before discussing the area for improvement.
5. First empathize, and then criticize. Reveal your own similar mistakes, and tell the individual what you did to correct them.
6. Check your intentions as to why you are engaging in the feedback process. Be clear that you genuinely want to help the person with whom you are speaking.
7. Use your human-relations skills. Do not order; instead make suggestions.
8. Show the benefit of changing the behavior.

9. End on a friendly note and agree on how to move forward.

Accepting Constructive Feedback

1. Stay calm and hear the person out.
2. Confirm your understanding of the situation.
3. Be open to self-improvement and change.
4. Trust that the person giving the feedback has good intentions.
5. Do not react defensively.
6. Don't offer excuses; just provide facts.
7. Thank the person for the feedback.
8. Agree on how to move forward.

Sum and Substance

> In our interaction with others we send signals and how those signals are received determines how we are perceived and how people remember us.
> A key ingredient in developing and maintaining strong interpersonal signals is self-confidence.
> First impressions are the most lasting. Since humans are very visual beings, more than half the impression we make is based on what people see.
> Our personal brand statement takes our individual skills and strengths and combines them with our interests. This identifies our unique promise of value to our clients, employees, colleagues, and other important contacts.
> Our business cards can reflect our individuality as well as the services we offer. Add a personal touch and be memorable.

> Making a good first impression is only the first step in creating for ourselves the professional demeanor that will determine how we are perceived by others. We must be constantly attentive when it comes to how we look, act, and interrelate with everybody we come in contact with.
> We create first impressions by how we use the telephone and manage our business correspondence.
> Successful people learn how to use their body language most effectively and how to read the body language of others.
> Make a point to listen attentively to others, whatever their rank, position, or level of importance may be.

2

DEVELOP YOUR PERSONAL
BRAND

To advance in our career, it is essential that we adhere to a set of standards. These standards will guide us in the way we live our lives and in the way we act and react in our jobs—our personal brand. Our image should be based on our personal brand. The signals we send to our bosses, subordinates, colleagues, customers, and everybody with whom we interact on the job should show that we are in alignment with our personal brand.

Vision and Mission Statements

Most major companies have both vision and mission statements. Just like a company develops its recognizable brand, our vision and mission statements can help us in developing our personal brand.

The most effective way I know to begin with the end in mind is to develop a personal mission statement or philosophy or creed. It focuses on what you want to be (character) and to do (contributions and achievements), and on the values or principles upon which being and doing are based.

Stephen Covey

Vision Statements

The typical vision statement embodies the ideal image of the organization or the team. It expresses the optimal goal and reason for existence. Unfortunately, few individuals take the time to create a vision statement for themselves. When developing a personal vision statement, think about what you would ultimately hope to accomplish as a result of your efforts. It is a big picture statement. You can obtain some guidelines in creating your vision statements by looking at those of some prominent companies.

Westin Hotels: "Year after year, Westin and its people will be regarded as the best and most sought after hotel and resort management group in North America."

Alcoa: "Our vision is to be the best company in the world—in the eyes of our customers, shareholders, communities, and people. We expect and demand the best we have to offer by always keeping Alcoa's values at the top of our minds."

General Motors: "Our vision is to be the world leader in transportation products and related services. We will earn our customers' enthusiasm through continuous improvement driven by the integrity, teamwork, and innovation of GM people."

IKEA: "Our vision is to create a better everyday life for many people. We make this possible by offering a wide range of well-designed, functional home furnishing products at prices so low that as many people as possible will be able to afford them."

Creating Our Personal Vision Statement

Many of us dream about what we would like to do with our lives. Few of us actually convert our dream into a personal vision statement. This does not mean that we should make every fantasy our vision. Unless we have very specific talents, it is unlikely our dream of making the winning touchdown in the Super Bowl, or starring in a hit movie should be our vision. We should build our vision on a realistic foundation within our capabilities. The vision statement may be career oriented or aimed on some other life purpose. A personal vision statement describes how we see ourselves in the future. It describes our hopes and dreams and evokes a sense of achievement and fulfilment.

Some examples are:

A graduating MBA student at Columbia University: "As I enter the world of business, I am committed to devoting all my time and energy to learning as much as possible about my job to become worthy of advancement in my career."

A fifty-year-old successful entrepreneur: "For the past twenty-five years I have devoted myself to becoming a successful and profitable business executive. My vision for the next phase of my life is to train others to replace me so that I can devote my time to philanthropic work."

A commercial artist: "To keep up with the technological changes in my field, I see myself learning and becoming an expert in computer applications that will enhance my artistic capabilities."

Mission Statements

The mission statement posits the implementation of the vision. It succinctly outlines what must happen for the organization, team, or individual to achieve the vision. This flows directly from the vision statement, and states how we will reach the vision. It should be specific, and therefore, unique to our organization, team, or ourselves. The mission statement should be easy to understand, realistic, and measurable.

Here are some examples of company mission statements:

Westin Hotels: "In order to realize our vision, our mission must be to exceed the expectations of our customers, who we define as guests, partners, and fellow employees."

FedEx: "FedEx is committed to our 'People-Service-Profit' philosophy. We will produce outstanding financial returns by providing totally reliable, competitively superior, global, air-ground transportation of high-priority goods and documents that require rapid, time-certain delivery."

Aflac: "To combine aggressive strategic marketing with quality products and services at competitive prices to provide the best insurance value for consumers."

Harley-Davidson: "We fulfill dreams through the experience of motorcycling, by providing to motorcyclists and to the general public an expanding line of motorcycles as well as branded products and services in selected market segments."

Microsoft: "At Microsoft, we work to help people and businesses throughout the world realize their full potential. This is our mission. Everything we do reflects this mission and the values that make it possible."

> *Everyone has his own specific vocation or mission in life. . . . Therein he cannot be replaced, nor can his life be repeated. Thus, everyone's task is as unique as is his specific opportunity to implement it.*
>
> *Victor Frankl,*
> *Philosopher and Author*

Creating Your Personal Mission Statements

In writing your own personal mission statement, be specific as to what you desire to accomplish. Consider action words to develop your mission statement.

- Encourage
- Collaborate
- Develop
- Produce
- Involve
- Support
- Change
- Emphasize
- Expand

Some examples of personal mission statements:

Dr Arthur R. Pell, human resources consultant and writer: "My goal is to enable people to develop a productive and rewarding life by teaching them the most effective approaches to self-development and interpersonal relations through my personal counseling, teaching, and writing."

Lisa Silverman, nutritionist: "I am committed to encouraging as many people as I can to change their eating habits to a well-balanced nutritional program through my newsletter, radio program, and personal counseling."

Larry MacDonald, marketing executive: "My mission is to advance in my career by using my creative skills to promote the products or services of my employers to expand their markets, increase their profits, and serve their customers in the most effective manner."

Write Your Statement

Before reading the balance of this chapter, take the time to create vision and mission statements that best reflect your personal image. After they are written:

1. Read them aloud. Are these true statements of how you see yourself?
2. Email the statements to several friends or colleagues who know your work for their review and comments.
3. Evaluate the reactions and make pertinent adjustments.

Live an Ethical Life

A key factor in your personal brand is your personal ethical code. It defines your standards of right and wrong. It helps one resist temptation and becomes the basis for making ethically sound decisions.

Our values determine what is good and what is bad. Our ethics determine *doing* what is good and *avoiding* what is bad. Ethics involve a set of standards that tell us how we should behave. No person with strong character lives without a code of ethics.

But ethics are more than what we *must* do. They're what we *should* do. Because acting honorably sometimes means not doing what we want to do. Ethics require self-control.

Ethics involve seeing the difference between right and wrong and a commitment to do what is right, good, and honorable. We must ask ourselves if we are willing to pay the price of making an unethical choice. Are we willing to sacrifice our pride, integrity, reputation, and honor by making an unethical choice?

> *From right understanding proceeds right thought; from right thought proceeds right speech; from right speech proceeds right action; from right action proceeds right livelihood; from right livelihood proceeds right effort; from right effort proceeds right awareness; from right awareness proceeds right concentration; from right concentration proceeds right wisdom; from right wisdom proceeds right liberation.*
>
> *Buddha's Path to Liberation*

Our Personal Code of Ethics

There is no limit to an ethical code—it can be as simple as one sentence or many paragraphs of personal thought and intent.

Here are some guidelines in developing our personal code of ethics:

1. Set reasonable boundaries of moral conduct. The key word is reasonable. Nobody likes rigid rules or guidelines.

2. Have a clear purpose behind the boundaries. Explain and reinforce the "why" behind the "what." "Because I said so," didn't work when we were children, and it doesn't work now either.

3. Communicate boundaries in a positive manner and keep the focus on what to do rather than what "not to do." For example, "keep confidences," rather than "don't gossip."

4. Give others an opportunity to contribute to the process of establishing appropriate boundaries in the workplace. Often, employees come up with stricter boundaries than managers.

5. Enforce boundaries and have the courage to stand behind them. Boundaries should be enforced consistently and fairly.

Ethical Decision Making

We make choices every day. Most of our day-to-day decisions don't necessarily involve right or wrong; rather they involve priorities, efficiency, planning, and managing resources. However, we also have to make those decisions that involve right and wrong within our ethical boundaries. These situations are often time pressured, emotional, and complicated. It becomes all too easy to be blindsided by temptation. We are often forced to make ethical choices reactively.

The middle of an ethically sensitive situation is the worst time to try to determine our ethical standards. We have to review the information, anticipate consequences, consider others, and manage our emotions; then act. Ethical decisions may happen quickly, but the consequences can last a lifetime. That's why careful consideration is important. A code of ethics can help. It determines direction in our lives.

We must think about the impact of the action on all of the stakeholders—all the people affected by a decision. Before we do anything, we must determine who is likely to be helped or harmed by the action under consideration. If someone will be harmed, how can we avoid or reduce the harm? Good questions to ask ourselves are, "What if the roles were reversed? How would I feel if I were in the shoes of one of the stakeholders?"

Our ethical code sets forth the ground rules for our life. Weigh choices and options to determine if they meet if ethical code or not. Clearly, actions that engender trust and respect, and that demonstrate a sense of responsibility, fairness, and community service, outrank and override actions driven by money, power or the desire for popularity. Similarly, actions taken with the long run in mind will frequently outrank those taken for more immediate returns. Ask "What are the possible consequences of my actions … both short-term and long-term?"

When faced with tough decisions, eliminate choices that conflict with our ethical values. Then, pick the most ethical option left. If you are still unsure of what to do in a particular situation, go with the choice that will produce the most good for the most people.

If you have clear values and standards, making decisions is easy.

Roy Disney

Evaluating Ethical Concerns

Too often we are under pressure to make decisions or take action. Under these circumstances, we may do so without giving full consideration to the ethical principles involved. Even if we have no qualms about a particular decision, it can be very helpful to take a moment to envision the action within the framework of others' values. Any or all of the following questions can help us think more clearly about whether a decision falls within our ethical code.

> Would we want our mom, dad, grandparent, or favorite relative to know what we are saying or doing?
> Would we want our child to know what we are saying or doing?
> How would our choice look on the front page of the local newspaper? Can we clearly and fully justify our thinking and our ethical choice?
> If, at the end of the day, a major portion of the population did what we are contemplating, would it be a good thing?
> Lastly, does the action comply the Golden Rule? Am I treating others the way that I want to be treated? TGR (The Golden Rule)—Treat others the way we want to be treated.

Living up to your ethical code will not only guide you in creating a strong personal brand, but it will also be a constant reminder to others that you act and work with integrity and honor.

Commit to Achieve

Part of the personal image projected by successful people is their commitment to achieve their goals. Most likely we make such a commitment, and even start to work toward it—but in a short time it is forgotten.

When Karen's boss announced that the company was going to install a new computer system, he offered anybody who wished to learn the system an opportunity to enroll in a training program. Being able to use the new system could give them much greater growth potential in the company. Karen registered for the course and attended the first two classes. When the program began to get more difficult, she found excuses for not attending and eventually dropped out.

Assuming that Karen *was* truly sincere in her desire to learn the new computer, what could she have done to assure that she would meet her goals—even when it became tougher than she thought it would be?

In order to assure that a goal will be met, we have to *commit ourselves to achieving it.* Commitment is more than just making a resolution. It is a solemn pledge that we will do all that we can to achieve our goal. It cannot be taken lightly. If you take your commitments seriously and follow the guidelines below, there is a strong chance that you will succeed.

Most of the important things in the world have been accomplished by people who have kept on trying when there seemed to be no hope at all.

Dale Carnegie

Set a Clear and Specific Final Goal

Instead of saying "I want to lose weight," set the exact number of pounds you wish to lose. In this way you can keep score and see day-by-day how close you are to reaching that goal.

When the goal cannot be quantified, make the targets as specific as you can, for example: "Be able to master Excel," or "Give a talk to my professional association."

Set Intermediate Goals

"The deadline for my report is March 30. By March 10, I will have completed all the preliminary research and by March 20, I will have the statistical analysis completed."

By setting intermediate goals, we make it easier to accomplish our overall goal. Take things one step at a time. Instead of worrying about meeting a thirty-day deadline, one should think in terms of meeting the deadline for the first phase and when that is accomplished, the next phase, and so on.

It also helps when you establish "control points." These are critical steps along the way by which you can measure the quality of your progress. In school, these control points may be quarterly or midterm exams. On a job they may be periodic performance reviews. In your commitment to achievement, you must set your own control points to examine how you are bringing excellence to your project. As we meet our intermediate goals, knowing that we're producing good quality work reinforces our commitment to continue. If our product is not as strong as we'd planned, our honest assessment as we go along helps us to determine what steps we can now take to get back on track.

Make a Contract

A contract is a binding agreement. When financial problems compelled Jason to leave college after his sophomore year, he made a commitment that he would get his degree within five years. He knew this meant taking night and weekend courses, spending a significant portion of his earnings on his education, and sacrificing most social and recreational aspects of his life. To assure that he would do this, he drew up a written contract with himself outlining his long term goal—to obtain his degree, and the intermediate goals: courses to be taken and when he expected to complete them. When difficulties arose or he was tempted to slacken his efforts, he would reread his contract and renew his commitment.

Share Your Commitment with Another Person

The great writer on self-motivation, Napoleon Hill, recommended that you share your commitments with another person. Jason gave a copy of his contract to his brother, Joe, who signed the contract as a witness and promised that he would see that Jason lived up to it. Over the next few years when, due to the pressures of the heavy load of work and school, Jason was tempted to drop courses, the support he received from Joe helped him keep his commitment.

Selecting the person or persons with whom you to share your commitment is important. You must choose somebody that you respect and do not want to disappoint. This person must be as enthusiastic about you reaching your goal as you are. If the goal is personal, it could be your spouse, a family member, or close friend. In a business situation, share your commitment with your mentor, a close colleague, a fellow member of a professional association, or even your boss.

Reward Yourself

When you have accomplished our goal, you have earned a significant reward. Max Harper quit smoking a dozen times, but he always started again within a few months. He made a commitment to stop permanently and promised himself that if he kept his commitment for one full year, he would buy himself a smartphone. By saving the money formerly spent on cigarettes, at the end of the year he had enough for the desired phone.

Knowing that they will give themselves a tangible reward in addition to the psychic satisfaction of meeting the goal helps some people adhere to their goals.

Committing ourselves to achievement is an important component of our personal brand. To achieve what you desire in life requires real commitment. By setting goals that are clear and specific, establishing intermediate steps so you can measure your progress, making a contract with yourself and sharing it with someone you respect and rewarding yourself when the objective is achieved, you will reach the goals that are important to you in your job and in every other aspect of your life.

It had long since come to my attention that people of accomplishment rarely sat back and let things happen to them. They went out and happened to things.

Eleanor Roosevelt

Generating Trust

Another component that makes up our personal brand is *trust*. Trust is defined as a firm belief or confidence in a person or thing. When we trust another person, an organization, or ourselves we possess an assured reliance on the character, ability, strength, or truth of that person or thing. Too little trust or too much trust can be dangerous. A healthy degree of trust is when we use a balance of head and gut, or facts and instinct, to make good decisions and exercise good judgment.

Trust men and they will be true to you; treat them greatly and they will show themselves great.

Ralph Waldo Emerson

It is always beneficial to an organization if the staff trusts the company and its management. In this day and age, loyalty to an employer is not a highly valued trait, and the more our employees trust in our integrity, the better are our chances of keeping them with us. In fact, research indicates that there is a considerable link between employee trust and profitability. Mutual trust between employees and employer is critical to increase the level of the organization's overall performance. Not only must we create trust in ourselves, but it is essential that we create and maintain a trustful environment.

The degree to which trust is an issue may be determined by some symptoms. For example, we may be showing some distrust in our organization if, depending on the day or the project, we may do the minimum to get by, lack motivation and commitment, avoid challenges, and appear to be "sleepwalking" through the day. If we have a more serious and ongoing trust issue, we may act out our unhappiness by demonstrating a negative attitude that affects others and results in diminished performance, absenteeism, and low morale. Employees who work in a highly distrustful environment tend to focus on problems, resist change, and undermine and sabotage their coworkers' accomplishments.

Benefits of a Trusting Work Environment

For many of us, how we perform in the first position to which we're promoted will define our future with the organization. Whether we are team leaders or department supervisors, a key function of our position will be to develop a motivated, productive team or department by building a trusting work environment. Doing so will lead to:

> Greater job satisfaction
> More committed and engaged employees
> Improved productivity
> Less stress
> A flow of innovative ideas
> Greater employee retention
> Better customer service
> Satisfied and loyal customers
> A confident staff

In almost every profession—whether it's law or journalism, finance or medicine or academia or running a small business—people rely on confidential communications to do their jobs. We count on the space of trust that confidentiality provides. When someone breaches that trust, we are all worse off for it.

Hillary Clinton

Principles for Building Trust

Here are some suggestions for building a trusting environment in the workplace:

1. Build rapport by taking others' interests to heart. Ask questions, learn what motivates them, and create an environment for growth and learning.

2. Listen sincerely with your ears, eyes, and heart—and without prejudice and judgment.

3. Honor and find merit in differences of opinion, biases, and diversity.

4. Ask. Don't tell. Collaborate with others in decisions, display an open and accepting attitude. Be receptive to new ideas, methods, and technologies.

5. Be willing to negotiate and compromise to achieve your goals.

6. Think before speaking. Consider the audience, relationship and environment when choosing your words and actions.

7. Think and speak in terms of "us." Use inclusive language and appropriate emotions. Communicate with diplomacy, tact, and sensitivity.

8. Take care of issues promptly. Speak confidently, decisively, and with authority. Offer evidence when stating opinions. Use instincts as well as facts to make sound decisions.

9. Demonstrate integrity. Stand up for your beliefs and values.

10. Remain humble. Be visible. Show your staff that you are "in the trenches" with them.

11. Be modest about your expertise and be willing to defer to the expertise of other competent participants.

12. Refrain from mood swings. Be patient and dependable. Act consistently and rationally and fairly. Be resilient and bounce back from disappointment.

13. Be a stellar role model. Act professionally and always walk the talk. Give others the benefit of the doubt.

14. Demonstrate respect, trust, and faith in others. Delegate and empower, and let go. Encourage risk taking and be available to help when needed.

15. Be authentic. Demonstrate congruency between your words and actions. Reveal your own feelings and thoughts openly and provide constructive feedback when necessary.

16. Be generous, courteous, approachable and available as a resource.

17. Be realistic when communicating vision, goals, and outcomes. Offer opportunities for growth, training, and mentoring.

18. Be human. Accept responsibility and admit mistakes, downfalls, and disadvantages.

19. Deal directly with others. Do not partake in gossip, spread rumors, or talk behind others' backs.

20. Support your staff. Focus on people's strengths, offer encouragement, and build their confidence. Show appreciation, give recognition, and share the glory by giving others credit for their accomplishments.

When Trust is Lost

No matter how committed we are when it comes to maintaining a trusting environment, there are times we may lose the trust of one or more people in our group. This may be the result of a misunderstanding, or more seriously, due to a poor decision or action on our part. We must take immediate action to restore trust.

Here are five steps to help reestablishing trust in the workplace:

1. Put your ego aside and allow yourself to be seen as vulnerable. We are human beings, not just authority figures.
2. Honestly review your perceptions and take full responsibility for your part in breaking the trust. Examine your assumptions and be honest with yourself. Reflect on what you may have done to lose the trust.
3. Meet privately with the individual and disclose your perceptions and concerns. Ask for their perspective. Keep an open mind, truly listen, and put yourself in their shoes.
4. Find out what that person needs from you to repair broken trust. Share what you need from them. Check for understanding and acceptance. Arrange to meet periodically to assess progress.
5. Be vigilant about upholding your end of the deal. Your actions will speak volumes.

We must open the doors of opportunity. But we must also equip our people to walk through those doors.

Lyndon B. Johnson

Our Personal Brand as a Leader

Another factor that contributes to our personal brand is our reputation as leader. As a supervisor, team leader, or mentor, how we manage new team members is crucial to the way in which we demonstrate our personal brand on the job.

You should make it a priority to help your new staff members get started on the job. The first day on the job can set the stage for success or failure, happiness or discontent, cooperation or rebellion. No matter how busy you may be, you should spend a significant amount of time with a new employee the day that person starts.

Develop Immediate Rapport

Plan for the arrival of the new person, and plan to spend at least two hours with him or her. Take him or her to lunch the first day. This is your chance to talk informally about the company and the department and also to learn about the new member of your group.

Introduce the new employee to other members of the department and to people in other departments with whom he or she will work. In making the introduction, always specify what kind of work that person does and indicate what your new employee will be doing.

"Marilyn, this is Gloria, our new market analyst. Gloria, Marilyn is in charge of our statistics section." In introducing Gloria to higher-ranking officials, follow company protocol regarding whether first names or more formal address is used. Even if you call your boss Don, if Gloria will be expected to refer to him as Mr Deane, then introduce him as Mr Deane.

Orientation

Many companies have formal orientation programs for new

staff members conducted by the human resources department. The orientation program usually covers such things as company history, discussions of the products or services provided, descriptions of benefits, and the like. In addition to this orientation program, as the immediate supervisor, one should discuss the mission of one's department and how it fits into the overall picture of the organization's workings.

It is important that a new person learn as soon as possible who is who in the department and the company. Using an organization chart helps, but often the organization chart does not tell the entire story. On the chart, Don Deane, Director of Marketing, is your boss. However, Don is about to retire and Ken Maynard, the National Sales Manager, is being groomed to replace him. This might be an important information for the new associate that would not be mentioned on a traditional chart.

Even more difficult to convey to a new employee is the corporate culture. Each company has developed over the years a philosophy, a special approach to dealing with problems, and a uniqueness that makes it the company that it has become. This "culture" is hard to put into words and often only can be absorbed by an employee over time. However, there are certain aspects of the corporate culture with which the new employee should be familiar from the beginning.

For example, Stew Leonard's supermarkets are dedicated to serving the customers. New employees are indoctrinated in this right from their first minutes on the job. In fact, this commandment is engraved in stone at the entrance of each store:

Rule 1. The customer is always right.

Rule 2. If in doubt, reread Rule 1.

One way to help an employee get started and learn the inner workings of the company is to assign one or, even better, two mentors to each new person, who will be available when you are not, to answer questions and guide them through the maze of company practices.

Above all, be a role model. Your associates look up to you for guidance. You must not only tell—you must do. Unless you walk the talk, your people will not trust you and your personal brand will be severely damaged.

Example is not the main thing in influencing others, it is the only thing.

Albert Schweitzer

Clear and Meaningful Job Descriptions

When mentoring a new staff member, a good start is to reread the job description for his or her position. Does it truly describe the job? If the new employee were to depend on this, could he or she do what is expected in that job? In many companies a job description may be written when the job was created and not changed in years. Most jobs are dynamic—they are always changing. It is important that all job descriptions be reviewed annually and adjusted to truly describe the work of the person holding that position.

Once the new employee has studied the job description, you should discuss it with him or her. Ask that person to describe how the job is perceived. A detailed discussion of the nature of the work will clarify any misunderstandings that may have arisen from just reading the job description.

Train, Train, Train

No matter how much experience a person has in a particular field, it is still important that one gives that person specific training in the methods and techniques that are used. In previous jobs, he or she may have done things somewhat differently, may have had less stringent standards, or may have faced different problems. The more time spent in training a staff member in the beginning of that person's tenure with the department, the fewer problems will arise later on.

Who should do the training? In some organizations special trainers are utilized, but in most companies supervisors train their own people. Because you are responsible for your staff members' work, it is important that you take a significant role in the training. However, it is not always possible for you to give the time needed for complete training, so other employees may be used to assist.

In choosing another person to help one train new people, one should adhere to the following guidelines:

› The trainer should be thoroughly familiar with the job.
› Teach the trainer how to train. Don't assume that because a person knows the job, he or she can train others.
› Be sure that the trainer has a strong positive attitude toward the company and the job. If we use a disgruntled employee to do the training, that person will inject the trainee with the virus of discontent.
› Periodically arrange a feedback meeting with new employees

to review what they have learned, where they need additional training, and to counsel them on how they can improve.

To get an employee started on the right foot and to assure that he or she will progress satisfactorily on the job, establish rapport immediately, orient carefully, train thoroughly, and give and get feedback regularly.

Sum and Substance

- The first step in developing your personal brand is to create a statement of your vision and your mission.
- A key factor in your personal brand is your personal ethical code. It defines the standards of right and wrong. It helps one resist temptation and becomes the basis for making ethically sound decisions.
- Part of the personal image projected by successful people is their commitment to achieve their goals.
- In order to assure that a goal will be met, we have to commit ourselves to achieving it. Commitment is more than just making a resolution. It is a solemn pledge.
- Guidelines for setting goals:
  - Make clear and specific goals
  - Set intermediate goals
  - Make a contract
  - Share your contract with another person
  - Reward yourself
- Trust is an important component of one's personal brand. Trust is defined as a firm belief or confidence in a person or group.
- No matter how committed you are to maintaining a trusting

environment, there are times you may lose the trust of one or more of people in the group. You must take immediate action to restore it.

➤ Your reputation as a leader is another factor that contributes to your personal brand. You may play a role as a supervisor, team leader, or as a mentor to a less experienced associate.

➤ One way to help an employee get started and learn the inner workings of the company is to assign a mentor to each new person, who will be available when you are not, to answer questions and guide them through the maze of company practices.

➤ No matter how much experience a person has in your field, it is still important that you give that person specific training in the methods and techniques you use.

3

··

YOUR PEOPLE MANAGEMENT
SKILLS

I n addition to developing the necessary personal skills
to advance in our careers, we must also learn the best
techniques of managing others. Staff supervision is often a
task that is a part and parcel of moving up the career ladder.

*Managers who successfully transition, increase their
contribution to the organization by 200–300 percent.*

Gene Dalton and Paul Thompson,
Harvard Business School

Worker versus Manager

You most likely have been promoted into management and
leadership positions because you were effective at what you

did in your previous job. Now, as a manager, your job is to get others to be able to do things as well as or better than you did.

Serving as a worker and serving as a manager require totally different skill sets. One's success requires making the transition from doing to leading in order to leverage one's skills and time.

Effective managers balance both the people and the process of the job. An emphasis on process may lead to the development of great systems, but such an emphasis may also result in a situation where no one understands them or wants to work within them. Process focus says: "Here's the plan and here's how we do things." On the other hand, focusing on people may result in everything coming to a stop if the people we depend upon leave our group. People focus says: "Let's discuss the plan and why we do things." With the right balance, both productivity and commitment stay at their highest levels.

In this chapter we will focus on people skills. Process skills will be discussed in Chapter 4.

Qualities of Outstanding Managers

Although individual strengths and abilities may vary, research indicates that outstanding managers view the world in similar ways. The following represent the most commonly observed qualities in great managers and leaders:

1. They hold strong values and high ethical standards.
2. They lead by example, acting with integrity in both their professional and personal lives.

3. They are knowledgeable about corporate and department goals and keep themselves informed of changes.

4. They develop a vision of the future, and are proactive and self-motivated to achieve results.

5. They are strong communicators and exceptional listeners.

6. They earn trust, credibility, and respect.

7. They are flexible under pressure and keep their emotions in check.

8. They invite constructive dissent and disagreement and are open to changes and new ideas.

9. They simplify ideas, concepts, and processes.

10. They nurture the concept of teamwork and respect diversity.

11. They take the time to get to know what drives individual team members and enjoy motivating them and helping them to succeed.

12. They recognize and maximize strengths in others.

13. They hold themselves and others accountable for results.

14. They are efficient and manage their time effectively.

15. They are creative and innovative.

16. They exhibit excellent judgment when solving problems, making decisions, and resolving conflicts.

17. They are committed to continuous learning and improvement.

Ten Common Mistakes of New Managers

Less experienced managers tend to make the same sorts of

mistakes as they learn the ropes. Watch out for these frequently made blunders:

1. Relying on their title to gain respect.
2. Contradicting themselves or breaking their word.
3. Taking work-related issues personally.
4. Treating all employees alike, rather than understanding the diverse qualities and motivating factors of every individual.
5. Setting goals without fully understanding corporate objectives and strategies.
6. Neglecting to plan and prioritize the goals of their department.
7. Failing to clearly communicate objectives and to gain consensus.
8. Continuing to do tasks that should be delegated.
9. Procrastinating rather than acting decisively when personnel changes are required.
10. Forgetting to show appreciation and recognition.

   Withhold not good from them to whom it is due, when it is in the power of thine hand to do it.

                                                            Proverbs 3:27

What Makes Employees Tick

As we move up the organizational hierarchy, our first priority is to recognize that our success depends on the success of the people we work with: our team, our department, and all the personnel with whom we interrelate.

The Gallop organization polled 400 companies on the retention of employees. It is found that an employee's relationship with his or her direct boss is more directly related to retention than to pay or job perks. Fair and inspiring leadership, including coaching and mentoring, retains employees. Another Gallop poll revealed that a key indicator of employee satisfaction and productivity is an employee's belief that the supervisor cares about the employee and can be trusted.

> *The conventional definition of management is getting work done through people, but real management is developing people through work.*
>
> *Agha Hasan Abedi,*
> *International Banker*

Stimulating and Fulfilling Work

An article in the American Society for Training & Development's October, 2003 newsletter suggested that in times of prosperity, stimulating and valuable work is more important to employees than salary and advancement. It's hard to put a price tag on enthusiasm and excitement for a job. Managers, who foster the involvement of employees and include them early on in projects obtain more creative ideas and create greater employee investment and pride in the outcome. Employees who actively participate in making decisions on a broad spectrum of issues help create an environment that they like and one in which they want to remain.

Growth Opportunities

By providing opportunities for growth, both personal and

professional, employees are less likely to look elsewhere. Providing training opportunities with respect to new skill and career development is an indication that a manager is willing to invest on behalf of the employee. This demonstration of interest in staff is key to employee retention. Encouraging employees to join professional organizations by paying membership fees and giving employees the time off and admission fees for attendance at lunches and conferences motivates them. Companies who have a high rate of employee retention hold a reputation for rewarding high performance by a jointly agreed upon career path (not necessarily direct advancement in the hierarchy), that gains the commitment of employees.

Respect the Need for a Balanced Life

Organizations that understand the significance of a balanced life have higher employee retention rates than those that believe that the employee should eat, breathe, and sleep work.

Acknowledging and respecting the importance of family and personal life of employees prevents burnout and fosters loyalty. Employers need to be aware of work-life issues. They must be sensitive to dual career, childcare, and challenges of being parents and whenever possible, be willing to offer flexible schedules.

Competitive Compensation and Benefits

Money is important, but it is for less important than we might think. Employees expect to be paid fairly and competitively. They feel entitled to benefits of health insurance, retirement funding, and the like.

The leader owes the follower productive conversations about the gifts that the follower brings to the organization and the kind of contributions the follower wishes to make—so that tasks can be designed that give the person hope.

Max DePree,
Chairman Emeritus, Herman Miller, Inc.

Leading Your Staff Members to Optimum Performance

Essential ingredients in obtaining the top performance of your staff members are to motivate and guide them—to make them feel excited and enthusiastic about their leader, about the company and the job.

Unfortunately, too great a percentage of the people in the work force are not enthusiastic about the work they do and the companies for which they work. Why should this be? From the first day on our very first job, somebody is always telling us what to do and what not to do. How often do we have the opportunity to have some control over our work life? If we would give our employees a greater voice in the way they do their work and encourage them to take charge of their jobs, they would put in more interest, more commitment, and get more enjoyment from their work…and their greater engagement will lead to higher productivity. Let's look at some examples.

Encourage Staff Members to Know Their Jobs

The first step in strong employee performance is knowledge. When people know their work well and perform it in a professional manner, they are on the track toward mastery of their work life. A perfect example of this is Nathan. When he was hired by his company, he was assigned to the mailroom as a messenger and clerk. He hated the work and was ready to quit. However, in the course of his job, he had to deliver materials to the computer department. He had some computer training in school and conversed with the people in this department about their work. Art, the computer supervisor, noted Nathan's interest in computers and requested his transfer to that department. Art encouraged Nathan to learn all he could about the equipment and software. In a few months, Nathan became as knowledgeable as anybody in the department. He loved his new job, felt comfortable and confident, won the respect of his coworkers, and became one of Art's most productive team members.

Aim for Excellence

Good supervisors work to get the best from their employees. Cathy knew that although Christine had been doing good work, she was not performing up to her potential. Cathy had to find a way to motivate her so that she could give an even better performance. She set up a meeting with Christine and told her: "Your work is good. I have no complaints about what you have been doing, but I know that you can do better. If you were less bright, I would be satisfied, but I see in you the capacity to be one of the very best people in this company. I'm confident that you can successfully aim higher. Let's you and I together work out a plan to help you achieve exactly what you are capable of."

Cathy and Christine together set goals and developed a

plan as to how they could be reached. Standards were set to measure how close Christine was getting to her goals. They met periodically to evaluate her progress. Within a few months, Christine was doing significantly more effective work and was on her way to a more exciting and valued career.

Encourage Participation

Behavioral scientists have advocated participative management for years. They have shown that when people participate in the decisions that affect their jobs, they are more likely to be committed to success.

One area in which workers can be particularly valuable is the establishment of quotas. In many jobs, quotas are an essential element. Factory workers are given quotas for hourly production; word processor operators are given quotas for pages generated per day; sales representatives for sales volume per month. Who usually establishes the quota? The boss. If the worker would participate in setting the quota, it would be far more effective.

When the supervisor told Jack he must produce one hundred units per hour with his equipment, Jack thought: "Ridiculous. Seventy, maybe. One hundred—never." But suppose the boss took a different approach: "Jack, our competitors are now manufacturing in foreign countries where the cost of labor is much lower than here. If we want to survive in this competition, we have to have more hourly production from each of our workers. How much do you think you can do?" Now Jack might think: "The survival of the company is at stake, and so is my job. I can do ninety units." Not only is Jack now motivated to produce more, but because the quota is a figure that he has set rather than his boss, his commitment to reach it is strong and genuine as it comes from within.

Encourage New Ideas

Most people feel they have some control over their jobs when the company takes their suggestions and ideas seriously. Nobody expects that all of his or her suggestions will be taken, but staff members do expect that they will be given serious consideration. We should instill in our employees an attitude of constructive discontent. No process or practice should be taken for granted. We have to eliminate the concept that if we always did it a certain way, it must continue to be done in that way.

We must always think about the future and encourage all of our staff members to think, think, think…and not just accept the status quo.

Suggestions should be evaluated objectively and, if viable, should be tried. Employees who suggest ideas should be given feedback as to how the ideas are working and rewarded when they are accepted.

If employees sincerely believe that they have some control over their jobs, they are going to make sure that the work goes smoothly and that they are successful in their endeavors. They will be more committed to excellent performance and will look forward to each workday with enthusiasm.

Different Strokes for Different Folks

A key ingredient in developing a highly motivated group

of people is to take the time to get to know each of them as individuals. Staff members are humans, not robots. Each member has his or her strengths and weaknesses, personal agenda, and style of working. Learning and understanding each person's individualities is essential to creating a motivated group of people.

As managers, one must develop the skills and abilities of each person in a group so that he or she can perform at top capacity. The best way to begin is to learn as much as one can about each person as an individual.

Knowing the people with whom you work requires more than just knowing their job skills. Sure, that's an important part, but it's only a part of their total makeup. Learn what's important to each person—his or her ambitions and goals, family, special concerns—in other words, know what makes each person tick.

Learn Each Person's Behavior Patterns

We all have a style or manner in which we do our work and the way we live our lives. Psychologists call this our "pattern of behavior." Study the way each of your employees operate, and you'll discover his or her pattern of behavior. For example, you might notice that Scott always ponders on a subject before commenting on it. Sheila rereads everything she's worked on several times before turning it in. Todd jumps into his work without much planning.

Getting to Know Our Associates

The best way to get to know people is to speak to them, ask

questions, and get their opinions on various matters. Maybe, we think that this is too intrusive. We don't want to be nosy. It isn't necessary to ask personal questions directly. By observing and listening, we can learn a great deal about our colleagues. Listen when they speak to you: listen to what they say, and listen to what they don't say. Listen when they speak to others.

Eavesdropping may not be polite, but we can learn a great deal. Observe how your associates do their work and how they act and react. It doesn't take long to identify their likes and dislikes, their quirks and eccentricities. By listening and observing, one can learn about the things that are important to each of them and the "hot buttons" that turn them on or off.

It's easy to remember these individual characteristics when one supervises a small number of people, but if you are involved with larger groups or have high turnover in the department then you should create a notebook or document with a page for each staff member, listing his or her spouse's name, children's names and ages, hobbies and interests, and any behavioral traits or facets of their personality to help you "reach" them.

Apply Motivational Techniques

Even after being trained in motivational techniques, many new managers find it difficult to implement them in their daily dealings with their staffs. Here are some suggestions on how to get started:

> Learn more about the individual goals and aspirations of each of your associates.
> Become more available to the people who report to you.

Rather than brush off their questions and suggestions, take the time to listen, evaluate, and respond to them.

> Overcome the temptation to make every decision. When asked for a decision, throw the problem back to the person asking, "What do you think should be done?"
> When new assignments are received, rather than planning the work yourself, enlist the participation of the entire group.
> Encourage associates to acquire skills outside their usual work duties. Use cross-training and assign them work that requires interaction with others in the group who have different skills and perform types of work.
> Confer with all staff members to ensure that they understand what is expected of them on the job and how their performance will be evaluated.
> Periodically hold exciting and productive department meetings.
> Visit suppliers and subcontractors and invite them to visit the company and attend meetings.

By following these suggestions, you will get positive results because of the increased productivity, improved quality, and enthusiastic cooperation and collaboration among our group members.

> *Good management consists of inspiring average people to do the work of superior people.*
>
> *John D. Rockefeller*

Enriching the Job

Although, there are many jobs that have the ingredients that lead to enjoyment and satisfaction, a large number of people have jobs that are monotonous and sometimes tedious. It's difficult, if not impossible, to generate excitement about these jobs.

One way to make dull jobs more "worker friendly" is to redesign them. Rather than look at a job as a series of tasks that must be performed, study it as a total process. Make the job less routine-based by enlarging its scope. Focus on what has to be accomplished rather than on the steps leading to its accomplishment by redesigning the manner in which the job is performed.

Here's an example of how job enrichment works. When Jennifer was hired to head the claims processing department at Liability Insurance Company, she inherited a department of disgruntled employees with low morale and a high turnover rate. The claims processing operation was an assembly line. Each clerk reviewed a section of the form and sent it to other clerks, each of whom reviewed another section. If errors were found, the form was sent to a specialist for handling. Efficient? Maybe, but it made the work dull and not very challenging.

Jennifer reorganized the process. She eliminated the assembly line and retrained each clerk to review the entire claim, correct any errors, and personally dealt with problems. Although operations slowed down during the transition, it paid off as the highly motivated team of workers found gratification in working through the entire process and seeing it completed satisfactorily. Production increased significantly and staff turnover in the department was reduced to a minimum.

When associates are trained to perform all aspects of the jobs their group handles, not only can any part of the work be assigned to any staff member (which gives us much more flexibility), but also, because associates do different work at different times. And because of that boring nature of the work is greatly lessened.

> *No one likes to feel that he or she is being sold something or told to do something. We much prefer to feel we are buying of our own accord or acting on our own ideas. We like to be consulted about our wishes, our wants, our thoughts.*

> *Dale Carnegie*

Avoid Negative Motivation

Threatening to fire people if they don't meet production standards or conform to company rules is sometimes effective— at least, temporarily. When jobs are scarce and people know that they won't have a job if they get fired, they do work. But how much work do they do? Some folks work just enough to keep from getting fired and not one bit more. This fear isn't real motivation; real motivation spurs people to produce more than just what's necessary to keep their jobs.

Fear of being fired becomes even less of a motivator as the job market expands. If comparable jobs are available in more amenable environments, why work for a dictator?

There are some people who do respond to negative motivation. Maybe they've been raised by intimidating parents or have worked under tyrannical bosses for so long that it's the only way of life they understand. Good leaders must recognize each person's individualities and adapt what they use to motivate that person to what works best for him or her.

Twenty-One Motivators That Really Work Well

Here are some of the best techniques for motivating people to commit themselves to superior performance:

1. Encourage participation in setting goals and determining how to reach them.
2. Keep all employees aware of how their job relates to others' jobs in the organization.
3. Provide all employees with the tools and training that's necessary to succeed.
4. Pay at least the going rate for jobs that are performed.
5. Provide good, safe working conditions.
6. Give clear directions that are easily understood and accepted.
7. Know each person's abilities and give assignments based on their ability to handle those assignments.
8. Allow people to make decisions related to their jobs.
9. Be accessible. Listen actively and empathically.
10. Give credit and praise for a job well done.
11. Give prompt and direct answers to questions.
12. Treat employees fairly and with respect and consideration.
13. Help out with work problems.
14. Encourage employees to acquire additional knowledge and skills.

15. Show interest and concern for people as individuals.
16. Learn employees' patterns of behavior and deal with them accordingly.
17. Make each person an integral part of the team.
18. Keep people challenged and excited by their work.
19. Consider associates' ideas and suggestions.
20. Keep people informed about how they're doing.
21. Encourage people to do their best and then support their efforts.

Recognition and Appreciation

Money—promises of raises or bonuses—is often the major motivator used by managers. Yes, some people are driven by financial incentives, but there are other forms of incentives that work even more effectively. In many surveys appreciation and involvement are cited more than money as a key factor in keeping employees happy. Recognition and appreciation of their achievements are powerful motivators. People need to be shown, verbally and nonverbally, that management respects their position and that they are important to the success of their organization. They enjoy both public and private celebrations of milestones and victories, and appreciate prompt and sincere recognition, be it verbal or written.

Too often we forget to express our appreciation to those who make our successes possible and our jobs more enjoyable. As managers we must make it a priority to let our staff members know we appreciate their contribution to meeting our objectives.

Look For Praiseworthy Situations

We tend to look for things to criticize rather than things to compliment when dealing with employees. We take our good workers for granted and never acknowledge them for their good work.

A good example is Doug, the owner of a supermarket chain. He told of his relationship with Tom, who managed one of his most productive stores. "Whenever I walked into that store I would find fault with everything Tom was doing. I expected him to run a perfect operation because I knew he could do it. When I really evaluated the store's progress, I noted that he had raised the volume $10,000 per week, moved from the red into the black and was well liked by his customers and employees. I had been so busy criticizing him I had never given him credit for what he had accomplished.

The next time I visited his store, we walked into the back room and I told him what a great job he was doing. I specifically commented on the increase in business and complimented him on his customer relations. He stood there—all six foot two of him, and tears came into his eyes. 'Boss,' he said, 'You have never talked to me like this in all the time I've worked here. I'm glad to know how you really feel about me.'"

Many business executives feel that an increase in salary or a bonus is sufficient indication of appreciation for a job well done. Timothy, the owner of a manufacturing plant, wanted to do more. One of his employees had consistently produced more than others. His bonus was more than the others received, but money did not express Timothy's gratitude, so he wrote him a personal letter of appreciation that he enclosed with the bonus check. In the letter he thanked him and told him how much he meant to the company. Later, the employee thanked him for writing it. He said it made him cry, and Timothy commented that it almost made him cry to hear him say that.

Virginia, head teller of a bank, makes a point of welcoming back employees who have been on vacation or out due to illness. She asks them about their vacation or the state of their health and brings them up-to-date on company news. She makes them feel that she missed them—and it comes across sincerely because she really does miss them.

Telling someone that he or she was missed, or that he or she is appreciated even when there is no special event, can be a rewarding experience for both the person receiving the appreciation and the person giving it.

Why do people fail to express appreciation? Perhaps we assume that appreciation is tacitly given when we don't criticize. Sometimes we feel it is not considered necessary because the other person is "just doing his or her job." Occasionally appreciation is not forthcoming because the person who should express it considers it a sign of weakness.

Reiterate Our Appreciation

One need not be effusive in expressing appreciation. A sincere acknowledgement of how you feel about the work done, the service rendered or the pride you have in a specific accomplishment is enough. Nobody ever tires of receiving honest appreciation. Assuming that your appreciation is implied without being expressed is short-changing the other person. Tell that person that you appreciate what has been done and why you feel that way. In situations where this is the result of a specific act, express your appreciation as soon as possible after the completion of the act. Like putting icing on a cake, your expression of appreciation will sweeten the joy of the accomplishment itself.

If your appreciation is for a continuing activity, periodic expressions of gratitude are appropriate. Just as telling your husband or wife from time to time how much your life together has meant to you and how you appreciate the little things he or she does to make life more pleasant will enrich a marriage, expressing appreciation to an associate will enrich the work environment.

Some people feel that by showing appreciation to others it may reflect on their own inadequacies. They subconsciously think: "If I tell them they did well, they (and others) may feel I am inferior to them." There is no basis for such a conclusion. All great people have repeatedly expressed their gratitude to those who have been helpful to them. In fact, it improves the image of strength they have earned and engenders a higher degree of loyalty among their followers.

Above All, Be Sincere

Appreciation must be sincere. One has to really feel and believe what he or she is saying for it to be perceived as genuine. Insincerity cannot be disguised by fancy words. Our voice, our eyes, and our body language all reflect our true feelings. There is no reason for one to fake expressions of appreciation. The realization that we owe so much to these people should tap the well of true and sincere gratitude that is deep in our hearts. Let it flow. Do not stifle it as it reaches your mouths. Let it spill forth into the ears of those who deserve it and their lives and yours as well will be a little better that day.

People aren't interested in how much you know, it's how much you care.

Howard Schultz,
Chairman, Starbucks

Sum and Substance

> As a manager, your job is to get others to be able to do things as well as or better than you did them.
> The Gallop organization found that an employee's relationship with his or her direct boss is more responsible for retention than pay or job perks.
> By providing opportunities for growth, both personal and professional, employees are less likely to look elsewhere for work.
> Surveys show that appreciation and involvement are cited more than money as key factors in keeping employees happy and productive.
> We all have a style or manner in the way we do our work and the way we live our lives. Psychologists call this our pattern of behavior. Study the way each of your employees operate, and you'll discover his or her pattern of behavior.
> One way to make dull jobs more "worker friendly" is to redesign them. Make the job less routine-based by enlarging its scope.
> Threatening to fire people for failure to perform is a poor

practice. Some folks will work just enough to keep from getting fired and not one bit more. Fear isn't real motivation; real motivation spurs people to produce more than just what's necessary to keep their jobs.

> Review the twenty-one motivators that really work well.
> Appreciation must be sincere. One has to really feel and believe what he or she is saying for it to come through as sincere.

4

....

ENHANCE YOUR PROCESS
MANAGEMENT SKILLS

In addition to perfecting your skills in dealing with people, potential managers must master the elements of learning the processes organizations undertake to succeed in achieving their goals. These include planning, delegation, time management, setting priorities, and encouraging innovation.

If we do not know to what port we are steering, no wind is favorable to us.

Seneca

The Planning Process

No work can be successfully accomplished without careful planning. In setting up your plan for any endeavor, you should:

1. Have a clear understanding of the goals you desire to accomplish.
2. Ensure that the goals are reasonable and achievable.
3. List what actions are required to attain your goals.
4. Appoint a specific person the responsibility of implementing the plan.
5. Commit the funds, equipment, personnel, and other resources needed to meet the goals.
6. Set performance standards against which you can measure progress toward attaining your objectives.

By taking the following steps your chances of success in achieving your plan will be facilitated:

Step 1: Define the Desired Outcome

The desired outcome is the result that you ultimately want. You should set forth how it will benefit your department or team, your clientele, and all others it encompasses. This should be clearly stated and agreed upon among senior management and others. If you have not done a good job of defining scope of the project, planning it will be almost impossible.

Step 2: Evaluate the Current Situation

Make a point of candidly looking at where you are today. What is the reality of the current situation? What factors help and hinder your efforts to carry out the project and its scope?

Step 3: Goals

Define and set realistic goals to successfully carry out the scope of the project. Without such goals, one drifts. Goals can be immediate, intermediate, and long-range. Achieving day-to-day goals (immediate goals) contributes to the achievement of intermediate and long-range goals. The acronym SMART can guide you in establishing your goals.

Goals should be:

- S = Specific in terms of processes and resources
- M = Measurable by objective data
- A = Attainable, in that they can be achieved
- R = Relevant to your vision
- T = Time specific with a deadline

Whatever failures I have known, whatever errors I have committed, whatever follies I have witnessed in private and public life, have been the consequence of action without thought.

Bernard Baruch,
Stockbroker, Advisor to Presidents

Step 4: Action Steps

In order to achieve goals, priorities must be established and specific action steps must be developed. These action steps should include:

- Requirements of the job
- Who will do the job
- Methods to be used
- Tying all the parts together to fit into the project
- Communication of results and format (written report, PowerPoint presentation, etc.)

Step 5: Cost

Determine the budget for, and cost of, each action step. Costs include:

- Personnel
- Material
- Time
- Overhead
- Miscellaneous

Step 6: Timetables

Deadlines should be set and communicated so there is a clear understanding of when the deadline will occur and what is due at that point. Doing so will ensure that immediate, intermediate, and long-range targets can be met. When establishing timetables, be realistic. Work backward from the project completion date to determine when each phase should be completed. Put the schedule in writing and distribute it to avoid misunderstandings.

Step 7: Implementation

An important, yet overlooked part of implementing a plan is making sure that all involved understand their roles in achieving the goals. Commitment to agreed-upon results must be established. Monitoring the implementation may result in modifying the scope of the plan and reevaluation of our goals.

Step 8: Follow-Up/Measurement

A critical part of the implementation process is to keep accurate records, analyze why deviations have occurred and take action to correct any challenges. Consistently monitoring the progress is critical to achieving your goal.

> *Being busy does not always mean real work. The object of all work is production or accomplishment and to either of these ends there must be forethought, system, planning, intelligence, and honest purpose, as well as perspiration. Seeming to do is not doing.*
>
> *Thomas A. Edison*

Delegate

There is no question that you and your department members have a lot of work to do. It is an essential tool of management to determine just what you will do yourself, and what will you assign to other people. When you delegate, you assign to staff members not only tasks, but also the power and the authority to accomplish them.

Effective delegation means that a supervisor has enough confidence in his or her staff members to know that they'll carry out an assignment satisfactorily and expeditiously.

Too often managers get bogged down in doing much more work than they should. Answer the following questions to see if you are overworking:

1. Do you take work home?
2. Do you still handle tasks you did before your promotion?
3. Are you frequently interrupted for advice or information?
4. Do you work out details others could handle?
5. Do you work on too many projects?

6. Are you frequently putting out fires and reacting to nonurgent matters?

7. Do you work longer hours than other managers in your workplace?

8. Do you spend time doing tasks for others that they could do themselves?

9. Are you overwhelmed with emails and voice mails after being out of the office for a few days?

10. Are you becoming involved in projects you thought you had given to someone else?

If you answered yes to these questions, you need to reassess your job and management of your workload. Chances are that you can delegate more work to your staff without a change in your department's performance.

> *The best executive is the one who has sense enough to pick good men to do what he wants done, and self-restraint enough to keep from meddling with them while they do it.*
>
> Theodore Roosevelt

Don't Hesitate to Delegate

You are responsible for everything that goes on in your department, but it is not possible, or even advantageous, to do everything yourself. Overwork can lead to burnout and ulcers, or even heart attacks and nervous breakdowns.

There are certain things, of course, that only you can do, decisions that only you can make, critical areas that only you can handle. Many of the activities you undertake, however, can and should be done by others.

Delegation enables one to assign the right work to the right person, helping both you and your associates use their skills and make contributions. This also ensures that all work gets done on time by the right person who has the right experience or interest.

If you have a difficult task, assign it to a capable, but lazy person. He or she will find an easy way to do it.

Anonymous

Giving Assignments

One should know the capabilities of one's associates. When you plan their assignments, consider which person can do which job most effectively. If you're not under time pressure, you can use the assignment to build up another person's skills. The more people who have the capability to take on a variety of assignments, the easier your job will be. If no one on your staff can do the work, then of course you will have to do it yourself, but make a point to train one or more employees in several tasks so that work on those tasks can be delegated in the future.

Make Sure the Instructions are Clearly Understood and Accepted

After you give detailed instructions to one of your staff members, you are likely to ask, "Do you understand?" And the usual answer is yes.

Yet does the employee really understand? Maybe. Perhaps that person isn't quite sure, but in good faith says "I understand." Or perhaps the person doesn't understand at all but is too embarrassed to say so.

Rather than asking "Do you understand?" ask "What are you going to do?" If the response indicates that one or more of your points isn't clear, we can clarify before the employee begins to perform the task improperly.

When it's essential for your delegatee to rigidly conform to your instructions, you must make sure that he or she thoroughly understands them. Give a quiz. Ask specific questions so that you completely agree about what he or she will do. When it's not essential for a delegated activity to be performed in a specific manner, you can just seek some general feedback.

Not only must all instructions be understood, but they must be also accepted by the delegatee. Suppose that on Tuesday morning, Janet, the office manager, gives an assignment to Jeremy with a deadline of 3:30 that afternoon. Jeremy looks at the amount of work involved and says to himself, "No way." It's unlikely that he will meet that deadline.

To gain acceptance, let the employee know just how important the work is. Janet might say, "Jeremy, this report must be on the director's desk when she comes in tomorrow morning. She needs it for an early morning meeting with the executive committee. When do you think I can have it?" Jeremy may think, "This is important. If I skip my break and don't call my girlfriend, I can get it done by 5:00."

Why did Janet originally indicate that she wanted the report by 3:30 when she didn't actually need it until the following morning? Maybe she thought that if she said 3:30, Jeremy would knock himself out and finish the report by the end of the day. But many people don't react positively to urgency. Faced with what they consider to be an unreasonable deadline, many people won't even try to meet it. By letting people set their own schedules within reasonable limits, you will get their full commitment to meeting or beating a deadline.

However, suppose that Janet really did need that report by 3:30, so that it could be proofread, photocopied, collated, and bound. To get the report completed on time, she could have assigned someone to help Jeremy, or asked him to work through his break that day.

Never tell people how to do things. Tell them what to do and they will surprise you with their ingenuity.

General George S Patton

Set Control Points

A control point is the point at which we stop a project, examine the work that has been completed, and correct any errors. Control points can help catch errors before they blow up into catastrophes.

A control point is not a surprise inspection. Employees should know exactly when each control point will occur and what should be accomplished by then.

One should not make decisions at every phase of an assignment and look over everyone's shoulders checking for dotted i's and crossed t's. When you micromanage, you stifle creativity and prevent team members from working up to their full potential.

No person will make a great business who wants to do it all himself or get all the credit.

Andrew Carnegie

Provide the Tools and Authority to Get the Job Done

A job can't be done without the proper tools. Providing equipment, reasonable timetables, and access to resources is an obvious step, but giving away authority is another story.

Many managers are reluctant to give up any of their authority. A job can be done without your micromanagement. You must give the people doing the job the power to make decisions.

If your employees need supplies or materials, allot them a budget so that they can order what they need without having to ask approval for every purchase. If a job might call for overtime work, give them the authority to order it. If you will be around to make every decision, the work will get bogged down, your staff members will feel disempowered and will likely lose their enthusiasm for the work.

Surround yourself with the best people you can find, delegate authority, and don't interfere.

Ronald Reagan

When We Delegate, We Don't Abdicate

Delegates almost always have questions, seek advice, and need our help. Be there for them, but don't let them throw the entire project back at you. Let them know that you are available to help, advise, and support them, but not to do their work.

When people bring you a problem, insist that they bring with it a suggested solution. At best, they will solve their own problems and not bother you. At the very least, they'll ask, "Do you think this solution will work?" which is much easier to respond to than "What do I do now?"

By following these suggestions for good delegation, you will be a more effective managers. You will accomplish more yourself because your staff members will be doing work more suitable for them and will improve their skills by getting experience that'd be important to their own development. Most importantly, it will give you time to hone your managerial skills.

Effective Time Management

Another important skill one must master as a manager is to manage your own time well. Unfortunately, failure to control time is one of the most common problems we face in meeting our goals.

To help you understand what might keep you from using your time effectively, rank the following list of items in order of biggest obstacle to smallest obstacle with number one being the biggest. Then determine what steps you need to take to overcome these obstacles.

	Ranking
• Lack of focus and motivation	_____
• Constant disruptions and interruptions	_____
• Too much to do in too little time	_____
• Too few resources to get the job done	_____
• Poor planning	_____
• Tendency to procrastinate	_____
• Inability to get organized or establish priorities	_____
• Inability to delegate effectively	_____

- Inability to make timely decisions   ————
- Time consumed by ineffective meetings   ————
- Stress   ————

> *It's not enough to be busy, so are the ants. The question is, what are we busy about?*
>
> *Henry David Thoreau*

Principles for Effective Time Management

Here are some suggestions on getting the most from your time:

1. Get your "house" in order. Clear the desk of clutter, and organize workspace and paperwork based on importance and frequency of use.

2. Use time-management tools such as to-do lists, batching tasks, time logs, project lists, priority lists, and calendars.

3. Post the to-do lists and priorities; reward yourself when tasks are completed.

4. Set realistic goals, break the goals into small steps, and dig in. Just start—you'll be surprised at how easy it is to finish.

5. Be efficient—plan each day by filling small gaps of time with small items on your to-do list.

6. Follow your internal clock. Some people are morning people and some are night people. If you are one of them, get things done when your energy and productivity level is at its highest. Create a schedule to take advantage of peak periods in the day.

7. When you find ourselves on a roll, take advantage of it. Capitalize on those spurts of energy, motivation, and creativity. These rolls can "cancel out" unproductive blocks of time.

8. Think to yourself, "Tomorrow I'm going on vacation and everything must be okay before I leave." Kick up productivity and get all urgent matters, phone calls, and emails done first.

9. Learn to make good decisions quickly.

10. Live in day-tight compartments, viewing each day as an opportunity to accomplish something important. Remove distractions, minimize interruptions, and get focused on the item or project at hand.

11. Use forced delays and breaks to your advantage, by getting re-energized and boosting your creativity.

12. Don't over commit. Don't volunteer to take on additional work, just say no—explanations are not always necessary.

13. Lose the "if I want a job done right, I have to do it myself" attitude. Delegate to others and trust them to do the job.

14. Adjust your attitude—set your alarm earlier and put enthusiasm in your work.

15. Go to business expositions and read trade magazines for time-saving ideas and technologies.

16. Learn from mistakes by determining what can be done differently the next time.

Take care of the minutes and the hours will take care of themselves.

Lord Chester

Use Monthly, Weekly, and Daily Time Logs

Here are some examples of time-management logs:

Monthly Project List	
For the month of_____	
I Plan to Do Fill in before month begins	Status Notes Fill in at the end of each month
Project 1: Actions to be taken % % %	Project 1: Accomplishments % % %
Project 2: Actions to be taken % % %	Project 2: Accomplishments % % %
Project 3: Actions to be taken % % %	Project 3: Accomplishments % % %

Add additional projects as needed.

Weekly Time Log

	Monday	Tuesday	Wednesday	Thursday	Friday
Pre 7:00–					
7:00–					
7:30–					
8:00–					
8:30–					
9:00–					
9:30–					
10:00–					
10:30–					
11:00–					
11:30–					
12:00–					
1:00–					
1:30–					
2:00–					
2:30–					
3:00–					

3:30–					
4:00–					
4:30–					
5:00–					
5:30–					
6:00–					
Post 6:30–					

Daily time log

Day of the Week: _____

Pre 7:00–	
7:00–	
7:30–	
8:00–	
8:30–	

9:00–	
9:30–	
10:00–	

10:30–	
11:00–	
11:30–	
12:00–	
1:00–	
1:30–	
2:00–	
2:30–	
3:00–	
3:30–	
4:00–	
4:30–	
5:00–	
5:30–	
6:00–	
Post 6:30–	

The Tyranny of the Urgent

One of the most common causes of failure to meet objectives is to confuse what is urgent with what is important. Crisis that develop must be addressed, but we must never lose sight of what is really essential for long-term success.

Some things are both urgent and important, such as dealing with major crises, meeting deadlines, resolving conflicts.

Some things that are important may not be urgent. Among these are project planning, clarifying values, building relationships, and developing skills.

Some things may be urgent but not important, such as phone calls, interruptions, emails, text messages, and the like.

Some things are neither urgent nor important, such as junk mail, busy work, engaging in personal matters on the computer.

Effective managers keep in mind the relevant urgency and importance of tasks as they utilize their time.

Prioritize

> *If you want to make good use of your time, you've got to know what's most important and then give it all you've got.*
>
> Lee Iacocca

You lead people and manage priorities to respond to the demands of your industry, customers, and the desired results. In a perfect world, time, cost, and quality would be equal.

But the reality of today's world is that we have to accomplish more—better, faster, and with less means—so prioritizing is a necessity. It is important to know what governs your world and if your boss, colleagues, and organization agree on what factor(s) dominate your business. This knowledge will help ensure that your priorities are in sync with those of the organization.

Here are some guidelines to help you in setting priorities:

> Prepare a to-do list.
> Arrange the list in order of importance to you, both personally and professionally.
> Consider how certain items on your list might affect others (for example, someone might need something from you in order to do his or her job).
> Indicate deadlines for each task.
> Be alert to consequences when deadlines are not achieved for specific tasks.
> Review the rewards for achievement of time-bound tasks.
> Delegate or eliminate items that remain at the bottom of the list. They probably are not worth your time.

Prioritizing "Hot Button" Concerns

Current research suggests that action-oriented leaders view their high-priority projects and goals—their "hot button" issues—in a very broad and strategic way. They can successfully communicate the current business context of the projects, the strategic role of the projects, and how stakeholders are impacted by the successful completion of the projects. They can succinctly explain where and how their projects relate to the organization's overall business strategy.

Some examples of hot button issues might be:

- Increased revenue
- Increased market share
- Improved customer satisfaction and retention
- Reduced costs

- Increased productivity
- Creative solutions to meet challenges

The Pareto Principle and the 80/20 Rule

In 1906, Italian economist Vilfredo Pareto created a formula to describe the unequal distribution of wealth in his country. Specifically, he observed that 20 percent of the people owned 80 percent of the wealth. (Of course, today in the United States, the numbers are even more askew.)

After Pareto made his observation and created his formula, others observed similar phenomena in their areas of expertise. Quality management pioneer, Dr,. Joseph Juran, recognized a universal principle that he called the "vital few and trivial many." Dr. Juran's observation led to the principle that 20 percent of something is, in general, responsible for 80 percent of the results. This became known as the Pareto Principle or the 80/20 Rule.

The following are examples of the 80/20 Rule:

> Twenty percent of stock takes up 80 percent of the warehouse.
> Eighty percent of sales come from 20 percent of the sales staff.
> Twenty percent of staff will cause 80 percent of the problems.
> Twenty percent of staff will provide 80 percent of production.
> Twenty percent of activities produce 80 percent of the results.

Of course, these figures are not necessarily applicable to any one set of circumstances in any one organization. But we can use the rule metaphorically to represent the common inequality in distribution and contribution. This concept can be a very useful tool to help effectively manage your time. It should serve as a daily reminder to focus the equivalent of 80 percent of your time and energy on the 20 percent of tasks that are really important.

Five Ways to Make an Immediate Impact

In most organizations, there is a lot of competition among well-qualified people for advancement in rank. A great way to give yourself a head start is to make an immediate impact on your organization's success.

Here are five ways to make a quick and positive impact.

1. Save money.– Continually looking for ways to save money without sacrificing the quality of goods and services is integral for every successful organization. If one can examine hidden costs and develop cost-cutting measures, overhead can be reduced and one's efforts will generate greater revenue. Get all team members on board for suggestions on ways to lower costs.

2. Save time.– Time is of the essence—and time is money. All savvy members of senior management understand that time is the scarcest of resources. If you can find ways to save time by streamlining processes and eliminating superfluous activities, you will be making an immediate impact.

3. Improve quality.– Asking for feedback from and listening to your customers and vendors can provide invaluable information for improving the quality of your goods and services. Surveys and assessments give us excellent insights

into how we can raise the bar and make an immediate impact.

4. Increase market share.– When we increase our customer base, we decrease our competition. Building trust, exceeding expectations, offering top-notch customer service, and asking for referrals are just some of the ways to increase sales and grow a business. You can make an immediate impact by increasing your market share.

5. Improve brand image.– Just about everything you do and say is a reflection of your brand image. From the demeanor of your sales staff and the layout of your marketing and collateral materials, to your customer service and quality, everything impacts your image. All successful companies have a strong brand image. They have succeeded at clearly differentiating themselves from the competition.

And an awareness of your competition is critical to your brand management. A simple Internet search on the industry in which your organization focuses is likely to turn up an abundance of information. Take note of your competitor's size, the scope of the services they provide, and geographic area they serve. Review their websites and take note of what makes them similar to or different from our company. Once you have gathered this information, you can determine what might be done to increase your organization's visibility in the industry by standing out from the others. You can make an immediate impact by continually looking for ways to improve your brand image.

SWOT Analysis

As candidates for advancement, you are constantly assessed by members of your organization. To keep ahead of the senior management's ideas about you, it is imperative that you carefully evaluate yourself on a regular basis. One tool is "SWOT" analysis. SWOT analysis is a tool used for understanding the Strengths, Weaknesses, Opportunities, and Threats we face when attempting to achieve a particular goal or outcome. It provides insight into the challenges one might encounter.

SWOT analysis enables us to focus on strengths, minimize weaknesses, and take the greatest possible advantage of opportunities available, and address threats.

Consider the following questions for identifying strengths:

What do you do exceptionally well? What advantages do you have?

What assets and resources do you have?

Consider the following questions for identifying weaknesses:

What could you do better?

What criticisms have you received? What are your vulnerabilities?

Consider asking the following questions to uncover threats to success:

What challenges might block your success? What is your plan to meet these challenges?

Identify opportunities by asking the following questions:

What opportunities do you know about?

Are you aware of trends on which you can capitalize? How can your strengths be utilized to ensure success?

The Innovation Process

For centuries, people have been fascinated by the creative process—the series of ordered steps through which a person or a group of people utilize the principles of creative thinking to analyze a problem or opportunity in a systematic, unbiased, and seemingly unconventional way. Some researchers have sought to uncover and understand what "makes" a person creative. Others have examined the kind of environment that stimulates creative effort and enables it to thrive. Still others have focused on the development of creative products and services. In recent times, modern research in the social and behavioral sciences has demystified the concept by showing how even modest powers of reasoning, analysis, and experimentation can help one attain insights into the nature of innovation and its many faces and expressions.

This increased awareness and understanding has captured the imagination of quality-conscious managers all over the world who have recognized the enormous benefits of developing the creative powers and problem-solving abilities of their associates.

In fact, surveys have shown that the ability to think creatively—to analyze problems and opportunities in new, innovative ways—is often thought to be one of the most valuable skills among managers within organizations committed to continuous improvement. Why? Because creative ideas result in new discoveries, better ways of doing things, reduced costs, and improved performance—issues vitally important to business people operating in modern competitive environments.

For these reasons, innovation must be considered a resource and managed like others—to the satisfaction of one's clientele.

You may say I'm a dreamer, but I'm not the only one. I hope someday you'll join us. And the world will live as one.

John Lennon

The Thinking Mechanism

The thinking mechanism of the human brain can be described as consisting of two sides: one part for uninhibited, creative thinking, and the other for analytical or judicial thinking.

Green-Light Thinking.– Over the years, the term "green-light thinking" has been applied to the thought process most conducive to the generation of creative ideas. In this instance, the quantity—not the quality—of ideas is emphasized. Green-light thinking includes:

- Deferred judgment
- Brainstorming
- Focus on quantity
- Idea fluency

The best way to have a good idea is to have a lot of ideas.

Dr. Linus Pauling

Red-Light Thinking.– The judicial part of the mind analyzes and evaluates ideas emanating from the creative, uninhibited side of the brain. Here the focus is on the quality of ideas. The term "red-light thinking" is often used to describe this process. This includes:

- Selective thinking

- Follows green-light thinking
- Focus on quality

Green-light and red-light thinking are two different processes and should always be separated.

Because most of our educational processes and systems have been devoted to developing the judicial thinking function (i.e., an ability to make decisions, compare and evaluate situations, distinguish between correct and incorrect, and the like). Most people have far more creative ability than they realize. In fact, potential can be developed to a much greater extent rather easily with proper coaching.

Developing Creative Abilities

Many of us do not think of ourselves as innovative. We think creativity is an inborn trait limited to people like Leonardo da Vinci, Thomas Edison, Bill Gates, or Steve Jobs. This is not the case. All of us have the ability to create.

Begin by looking for any product, service, or situation where the following innovation process can be utilized as a problem-solving or opportunity-exploring tool. The process should be employed with an attitude of constructive discontent, that is, you should look at your business processes and products with a productively critical eye. The series of steps that follow are designed to help you see your business anew.

Step 1: Visualization

What is your goal or objective? Create a picture of what you want the outcome to be and develop a vision of what the ideal situation will look like. Whether this is a problem that can be overcome or an opportunity for improvement, the visualization process will help set the scene and motivate you for moving forward.

Step 2: Fact Finding

Get the right facts. Look at the "who," "what," "when," "where," "why," and "how" of situations. Whether positive or negative, these details must be factual. We defer judgment about the facts and simply accumulate them. Once collected, the facts that we've accumulated are "symptoms" or "causes" that when eliminated, will lead to the resolution of the challenges. We must keep in mind that the "right solution to the wrong problem is more dangerous than the wrong solution to the right problem." When properly identified, opportunities and/or problems can then be prioritized.

Step 3: Opportunity Finding

The way you state the opportunity will dictate whether you get creative or judgmental input. Your objective is to defer judgment and avoid mental or verbal "finger pointing." Therefore, the opportunity should be phrased in the form of this question: "In what ways can we...?" For example, "In what ways can we increase sales?" or "In what ways can we decrease costs?"

Step 4: Idea Finding

Idea finding can be done on an individual basis or in a group. Group participation is popularly labeled "brainstorming." No judgmental thinking is permitted at this stage.

To ensure that you drive out self-censorship (driven by

the fear of embarrassment), participants should be required to write before they speak. Writing out ideas allows people to concentrate on quantity versus quality. It allows "idea fluency" without group members reacting to others' opinions, ideas, or personalities.

Step 5: Solution Finding

Judicial thinking takes place in the solution-finding step, where we evaluate the ideas produced in the green-light thinking step. After sufficient writing has taken place, the facilitator should ask the participants to determine their "best" and "silliest" ideas. In the discussion of the "best" ideas, the facilitator should let others speak first so as to avoid tainting the process. During discussion of the "silliest" ideas, the facilitator should go first to ensure that the participants won't self-censor. Defer judgment, strive for quantity, and stimulate deriving new ideas from those offered.

Based on the ideas that have been generated, you can then ask yourself: "What criteria must these solutions fit within? What criteria must we absolutely have as a result?" Determining absolute and desirable criteria makes the decision-making process more objective and less personal.

Step 6: Acceptance Finding

Unless you are going to personally implement the solution, you may have to get other people involved, and that may be a whole new challenge. You must anticipate objections to your idea and perhaps restart the process again at the Opportunity Finding stage (i.e., "In what way can we get buy-in?"). The innovation process is therefore, often not a linear technique; one solution may become a new problem.

Step 7: Implementation

In the green-light thinking and red-light thinking steps, you identified ideas and solutions. Now you need to put them into action. Set up a time frame—listing each phase of the project to its completion.

Step 8: Follow-up

By following up, you assure that you are staying on track. Schedule follow-up meetings will probably occur in thirty and sixty days, or some other time frame that is appropriate to the project's progress. Don't put off what you have started. Keep the energy and motivation going.

Step 9: Evaluation

It's always useful to reflect back and consider whether our efforts have been fruitful. Have we achieved the result we had hoped for? Did things seem to fall into place? This last step is the "tell-all" for the process.

> *Capital isn't so important in business. Experience isn't so important. You can get both these things. What is important is ideas. If you have ideas, you have the main asset you need, and there isn't any limit to what you can do with your business and your life.*
>
> *Harvey Firestone*

Building Group Participation

We cannot fine-tune our organization's processes by ourselves. Successful leaders not only encourage participation of their associates in developing innovation, but also make it an integral component of their jobs.

Some suggestions to help build a participative group include:

› Develop an environment that encourages ideas.
› Let all participants study the problem or opportunity in advance of the session.
› Keep sessions within twenty to thirty minutes.
› Encourage every participant to offer ideas, no matter how irrelevant or silly they may seem to be. What appear to be poor ideas may spark more significant ideas in the minds of other participants.
› Do not "red-light" any ideas offered.
› Never evaluate any of the answers; remain neutral.
› Do not give your ideas at the meeting.
› Encourage innovative thinking.
› Urge participants to "hitchhike" or build on the ideas of others.
› Strive for a quantity of ideas.
› Allow each concept to provide the basis to consider all related or similar ideas.
› Discourage participants from evaluating the ideas.
› Discourage participants from "selling" the ideas.
› Record every given answer.
› Review the list.
› Allow people to add to the list.
› Get a copy to all participants within a week of the meeting.

Sum and Substance

> No work can be successfully accomplished without careful planning.

> The eight steps to effective planning are:

  1. Clearly state what you want to accomplish.

  2. Evaluate the current situation.

  3. Set immediate, intermediate and long-range goals.

  4. Determine the action to be taken.

  5. Analyze the cost—set budgets for project.

  6. Timetables—set a timetable for when each phase should be completed.

  7. Get commitment from all participants to best ensure the plan's implementation.

  8. Follow up—analyze deviations and correct them.

> You cannot do most projects all by ourselves. Assign phases to qualified staff members and give them the authority and power to accomplish them.

> When delegating assignments, make sure the instructions are clearly understood and accepted.

> Set control points so that you catch errors before they blow up into catastrophes.

> Delegates almost always have questions, seek advice, and need your help. Let them know that you're available to help, advise, and support, but not to do their work.

> Managers must manage their time effectively. Review the sixteen time-savers listed in this chapter.

> Use monthly, weekly and daily time logs.

- To make most effective use of your time, you've got to know and then prioritize what's most important.
- When setting our priorities consider the "hot buttons,"— those issues of top concern to senior management and other stakeholders.
- Five ways to make an immediate impact are:
    1. Save money.
    2. Save time.
    3. Improve quality.
    4. Increase market share.
    5. Improve brand image.
- The ability to innovate, to create new products or systems, and to evolve existing products, services, or systems, is an asset that senior managers look for in advancing managers.
- The thinking mechanism of the human brain can be described as consisting of two sides: one part for uninhibited, creative thinking (green-light thinking) and the other for analytical or judicial thinking (red-light thinking).
- All of us have the ability to create. Begin by looking for any product, service, or situation where the innovation process can be utilized as a problem-solving or opportunity-exploring tool.
- Encourage your staff to be innovators by establishing a creative, cooperative, and supportive environment always open to new ideas and concepts.

5

....

ENHANCE YOUR PUBLIC
SPEAKING SKILLS

L eaders must be excellent communicators. A significant part of your training for advancement is the ability to present your ideas to others both orally and in writing and to take in input from them. In this chapter we discuss how to work on your public speaking techniques. In the following chapter we will address your writing skills.

Presentations to Inform

The most common type of business presentation is the presentation to inform. Every week in our careers, perhaps even every day, we listen to presenters give us information ranging from status reports to procedural guidelines to policy changes. For many of us, the majority of the presentations that we give fall into the informative category, in one way or another.

As leaders you will be required to make many presentations in a variety of situations. These include:

> Training sessions
> Sales meeting/Staff meeting updates
> Project status presentations
> Financial results presentations
> Product/Project launches
> Technical presentations
> Orientation sessions
> Addresses to professional and trade associations
> Addresses to chambers of commerce, service clubs, and community organizations

Some individuals are very competent in giving clear presentations to inform. Leave the presentation with a clear understanding of the message, the desired end result, and key points that you need to remember. On the other hand, many presentations are disorganized, hard to follow, and one leaves with only a vague idea of the point of the presentation.

As you prepare yourself to move into management positions, you must learn the step-by-step approach to these presentations so that you can be sure that your message will be clear, your audience would stay engaged, and you'd cover all the relevant points you wish to make.

Everything that can be thought at all, can be thought clearly. Anything that can be said, can be said clearly.

Ludwig Wittgenstein

Presentation Planning Assessment

To assess the way you currently deliver presentations to inform, answer the following questions using 'A' for always, 'S' for sometimes, and 'N' for never.

1. I carefully plan how to deliver my information. _____

2. I use supporting visual aids to make my message easier to understand. _____

3. I prepare handouts or a powerpoint presentation to reinforce my message. _____

4. I conduct question and answer sessions after delivering information. _____

5. I follow up to make sure that listeners understood my message. _____

6. I solicit feedback to see how well I communicated my message. _____

7. I practice my presentations before delivering them. _____

8. I use a structured approach to preparing my message. _____

9. I research evidence to make my message more convincing._____

10. I use examples and illustrations to be more interesting._____

11. I narrow the content down to the most relevant information._____

12. I frequently summarize to keep my audience on track._____

13. I get feedback from my colleagues on my presentations._____

14. My audience stays engaged when I am presenting information._____

15. I am able to give a presentation with energy and enthusiasm._____

Your goal is to be able to train yourself to respond with an 'A' to all these questions.

Who is Your Audience?

Professional presenters take their audience into consideration when planning a presentation to inform. One of the major challenges of this type of presentation is making sure that we are not speaking above or below the level of knowledge and expertise in your audience. Many audiences will hold individuals with diverse levels of experience, which will make your task even more challenging.

When planning to give an informational presentation, you should do your best to learn as much as possible about your audience's familiarity with the subject.

> How educated is this audience on the topic of my presentation?
> Am I talking, for example, to engineers or end users, or both?
> Do I need to provide extensive background information to put my topic into perspective, or is this audience knowledgeable about the context of my message?
> What previous experience or education have the audience members had with the topic?
> Is this topic something they deal with every day or week, or is it new to them?
> If they are experienced with the topic, what kinds of issues

or concerns have arisen in the past that they would like to see addressed?

> Do we have any reason to believe that the audience has a strong feeling about the topic of our presentation?
> If issues exist, what kinds of attitude are reflected in this audience?
> What problems or criticisms have arisen with this audience concerning my topic?
> What personalities will be present that may carry personal bias for or against my key messages?
> Is this a group that needs all the detail I can provide, or are they just looking for a summary of the topic?
> How much will this group be impacted by my message? How much will I be asking them to change what they are already doing?
> Are there safety or policy issues in my message that require detailed information for the audience?

Planning Your Presentation

The purpose of your presentation is to communicate information. Your goal is to get this information across to your audience in an interesting, engaging, and professional way.

Listeners appreciate brief, organized presentations that get to the major points quickly and clearly.

In planning the presentation there are five critical elements for success, easily remembered as the LIONS formula:

- **L**anguage that is easily understood
- **I**llustrations and examples
- **O**rganize ideas carefully

- **N**arrow presentation focus
- **S**ummarize

Language That is Easily Understood

Don't assume that the audience is familiar with industry or company jargon, abbreviations, or slang. It takes little time to briefly define terms as we present. If you commit to using actual words, rather than acronyms or abbreviations, you need to make sure that everyone in the audience will understand your message.

Illustrations and Examples

Presentations to inform that are heavy with facts and figures can really test the attention span of an audience. By using a real-world example, a relevant story, or a PowerPoint slide with photographs or charts, will break up the monotony and engage the listeners.

Organize Ideas Carefully

Everyone has had the experience of listening to presenters who have not thought through and organized their material, so they jump from point to point randomly, leaving the audience confused and disengaged. Take the time to organize material so that it is logical and easy to follow.

Narrow Presentation Focus

Unless you are conducting training session in which detailed directions may be necessary, most audiences don't need all the facts and figures, just those that are relevant to them. The challenge is finding a way to narrow subject matter to the specific presentation and give the audience enough information, and no more, within the allotted time frame.

Summarize

End the presentation by summarizing the major points, especially the desired end result. This leaves the audience with a final impression that is clear and memorable. If transitioning into a question and answer session, repeat the summary after the Q and A.

> *Many talks fail to be clear because the speaker is intent on establishing a world record for ground covered in the allotted time.*
>
> *Dale Carnegie*

Structuring the Presentation

An innovative presentation will keep the audience intrigued, but it's best to save the innovation for the subject matter. In terms of how you make your presentation, following a traditional structure helps to ensure your success.

Opening: Statement of Topic

Your opening statement in which you lay forth the topic should be brief and clear. It should leave no question in the listeners' minds as to the subject matter of the presentation. This is especially true when the presentation is part of a longer series of presentations, such as a staff meeting or full-day training session.

State Key Message: Desired End Result

Your key message statement should give the audience a clear picture of the main message of our presentation. It is simple, direct, and tells the audience where you are going with the information. It should answer this question in your audience's mind: "Why should I listen to this presentation?"

Present Key Points and Results Expected

You should follow your key message statement with the key points you will make and the expected results, in straightforward language. In general, the fewer words, the better when stating your points/expected results. To emphasize the key message of your presentation to inform, we succinctly restate the key message or the desired end result of your presentation. This leaves the listeners with a message that they will remember long after the presentation.

Types of Evidence

Once you have told your audience what you want to convey, you must present evidence to support it. There are several forms of evidence you could use. You can identify various types of evidence by using the acronym *DEFEATS*:

- **D**emonstrations
- **E**xamples
- **F**acts
- **E**xhibits
- **A**nalogies
- **T**estimonials
- **S**tatistics

Your presentation will be more interesting and persuasive if you use a variety of types of evidence to support your message.

Closing

Restate the key message. Reiterate what you want the participants to do:

- Take a specific action.
- Practice a new technique.
- Prepare a plan to implement the points discussed.
- Train their subordinates in the areas covered in the talk.
- Other pertinent action.

As you conclude, thank your audience members for their attention and commitment.

Think as wise men do, but speak as the common people do.

Aristotle

Using Visual Aids to Reinforce Your Message

Presentations are more interesting and engaging when you find ways to use visual aids to make your point. Turning data into a graph or chart makes your message more quickly and easily understood. Diagrams and photographs pull the listeners attention to the presentation. Consider handouts as a way to make information accessible to the audience after a presentation.

Visuals can also be used in one-to-one communication. In training her people to handle insurance claims, Joan found that the process was much more easily understood when she drew a flow chart as she described it. As she taught each phase, she outlined it by drawing boxes for each step and arrows showing the movement from step to step.

Steve learned from difficult experience that telling his people how to do the job was not enough. Unless he brought his trainees from place to place in the warehouse, they had difficulty in understanding what he was teaching. This was a very time consuming effort. He simplified the training by designing a model of the storerooms with which he could orient his people as he told them about the work they would be doing.

Many executives have flip charts or chalkboards in their offices so that they can use visual means to enhance their oral communications. By illustrating the subjects discussed with charts, graphs, diagrams, or sketches, what is being presented becomes far more effective. People tend to learn faster and remember longer a subject in which the listening is augmented by visual images.

One of the most popular professors at Syracuse University, School of Journalism was also a cartoonist. He drew cartoons and caricatures as he lectured. His colleagues scoffed at this practice and considered it very unprofessional. "He's just amusing his classes, not teaching," they claimed. Yes, his students did find it amusing, but they absorbed a great deal more information than they would from the lectures alone. Years later, his students could still recall his teachings.

There are many forms of visual aids. Among these are:

> Charts
> Graphs

- › Photographs
- › Diagrams
- › Handouts
- › Working models
- › Videos

Presentation Formats for Visual Aids

The format we use in showing our visuals depends on the type of visual and the size of the audience. For small groups, charts, graphs, diagrams, and the like can be posted on the walls of the room or displayed on an easel. Videos could be shown on a small TV screen or on as a power point on a laptop or desk computer. Chalkboards can be used where appropriate.

For larger audiences, charts, graphs, photos and related material can be shown as Powerpoint slides. Videos or slides can be projected on a large screen. Statistical tables and charts showing large sets of numbers are best presented as handouts.

Soliciting Feedback

Business professionals look for ways to get feedback on the clarity and relevance of their presentations to inform. Some of the ways that you can receive feedback include:

Conduct a Q and A Session

The questions that are asked by the audience tell us whether our message was clear. It's the most immediate way to get feedback from the listeners. If there are questions that indicate a lack of clarity, you can take the opportunity to restate your point, and perhaps offer additional evidence to support your message.

Follow Up with a Survey

Surveys maybe distributed at the end of the presentation itself or as a follow-up. Email surveys allow time for the presentation to be processed by the participants before making an evaluation of your message.

Ask for a Detailed Evaluation

Before the presentation, ask specific people if they would be willing to give you feedback after your presentation. Tell them your goals in the presentation and the skills you are trying to improve. Ask for ways to make the message easier to understand and the ways in which you can enhance your performance in future presentations. In considering the responses, look for suggestions that you can express visually, such as with charts or graphs.

Test for Knowledge

"Testing" the audience to see whether you've successfully conveyed your message can be done in several ways. One is to question the group at the end of the presentation to see how well they remember our key information. Another way is to create a test that will assess the retention of our message with the listeners. Other ways include follow-up telephone calls or e-mails.

Presentations to Gain Input

Rather than making a presentation to give information, sometimes the objective is to obtain information. To be effective, your approach to this type of presentation will be somewhat different.

Know Your Audience

When planning a presentation to gain input it is essential to consider the people from whom we wish to get this input. You must know as much as you can about the people in the group you are addressing. Some of the things you must learn about our audience are:

Knowledge of the Topic

To gain input, we typically include participants with a thorough knowledge of the topic. Sometimes, however, we may want an audience that has little or no experience with the topic, as in focus groups or market research.

Previous Experience with the Topic

Does the audience include individuals who have had a range of experience with the topic? If so, how have they reacted, positively or negatively? What is the extent of this experience?

Level of Preparation Required for the Meeting

If you are looking for informed input, you may need to ask the participants to do some work prior to the meeting. Consider what they may need to bring with them to the presentation in the way of documentation, homework, research, or planning.

Individual Bias Concerning the Topic

Are you aware of bias for or against the topic? Does this audience include individuals either who champion this topic or who are antagonistic toward some aspect of it?

Attitude of Open-Mindedness and Cooperation

Review the individuals participating in the presentation. Do they include people who are open about exchanging their ideas and opinions? Are there participants who are reluctant to speak up? Will this audience cooperate with the agenda and purpose?

Degree of Detail Preferred by Participants

Some audiences want only the basics about the topic under discussion. Others need more details before they are willing to express themselves. Consider preparing levels of detail from broad to specific that you can bring into the discussion as needed.

Supporting Evidence

You must be prepared to present basic evidence in the body of your presentation and to have available additional evidence in response to questions and requests for clarification.

Your Audience's Expectations

In order to get the most participation from the audience, you must know what they want from you. Some of their expectations are likely to include:

➤ An organized agenda.
➤ An understanding of the benefits to them of exchanging their ideas.
➤ A clear understanding of your aim.
➤ Concise facilitation of the presentation.
➤ A facilitator who keeps the discussion under control and focused.

Planning the Presentation

The presentation to gain input is used when your primary goal is to set a subject before a group in order to get their suggestions and opinions into the open. The more clearly you present the issue under discussion, the more targeted your audience's input will be.

Typical presentations to gain input include:

> Brainstorming sessions
> Focus groups
> Process analysis meetings
> Problem-solving meetings
> Strategic planning sessions

Planning for a presentation to gain input is different from a presentation to inform or to persuade. There are additional considerations that you have to take into account when you ask the audience to exchange ideas. Some of these considerations include:

• *Possible Resistance to Candor*

Some individuals are reluctant to share their opinions and ideas. Reasons for this can range from lack of confidence in their ideas or their ability to express them, lack of experience with the topic under discussion, or simply personality type. You should also bear in mind that in a corporate setting, staff members might be reluctant to express a displeasure with the organization or the way something is done. You may want to assure your audience members that honesty on their part will not result in any type of retaliatory treatment.

- *Overcoming a Lack of Interest in Your Topic*

The participants, like you, have busy schedules with multiple priorities. There is a chance that your topic does not seem like a priority to some participants and, as a result, they are uninterested and disengaged.

- *Unprepared Participants*

Ideally, you have informed your participants ahead of the meeting about your proposed discussion, and have asked them to come prepared to discuss it with examples, experiences, and research. Sometimes your audience will go to this trouble, and sometimes they come to the meeting with little or no advance preparation. You must be ready to summarize the topic for an audience that is not prepared for your presentation.

Four Planning Analysis

In order to help the plan presentation, you should determine:

1. What is the audience's current situation in relation to my topic? Is the topic a hot issue with this audience? What experience have they had with the subject under discussion? Are there any situations that have occurred that are likely to affect their input?

2. What are the challenges that the audience members are facing? If the topic is one that has created concerns for this audience, what are they? Find examples of those issues before the presentation, and prepare so that you are able to respond appropriately.

3. What do that audience members consider to be important

or unimportant concerning the topic? Prior to the presentation, talk to selected participants to see how they feel about the subject under discussion. If you are giving the same presentation to several different audiences, you can expect that some will consider the topic to be more important than others.

4. What will be the benefit to this audience if its members are persuaded to exchange their ideas and opinions? It's easy for the listeners to stay in the background and wait for the discussion to run its course, while contributing little or nothing. Think of compelling reasons why it is in their best interests to share their ideas and get a favorable outcome to the discussion.

Structure

Presentations to obtain information should be structured as follows:

1. Statement of the issue under discussion
2. Description of possible solutions, with advantages and disadvantages of each solution
3. Question to see if there are additional solutions that should be considered
4. Open up the presentation to a discussion of the proposed solutions
5. Wrap-up

Sample Presentation to Gain Input

The following text is a short sample of the "script" for a presentation to gain input.

Opening—Statement of the Issue Under Discussion

"As most of you know, you will be remodelling your offices over the next two months, which means that you will have to move to temporary offices for several weeks. We are looking for your input on the best way to make this process efficient and to continue to provide services to our customers."

Possible Solutions with Advantages and Disadvantages

"We are considering two possible ways of doing this move. Our first proposed solution is to move the administration, finance, and HR personnel to the manufacturing facility for two months.

The advantages of this solution are that everyone would be in proximity to one another, and you all could easily communicate under one roof.

The disadvantages are that the space is limited there, and we would be very crowded."

"Our second proposed solution is to go to a virtual office for the next two months, and have everyone work from home as much as possible.

The advantages of this solution are that you would not have to move everything twice, and employees who live a long way from the manufacturing facility would not have to commute.

The disadvantages are that every Wednesday you'd still have to come in for the teleconference with the Barcelona office, and you'd have to get rides or use public transit, as the construction crew will be occupying the parking lot."

Seek Additional Solutions

"Who would like to add to these two suggestions?"

Initiate Discussion of Solutions

Briefly summarize the options presented and then open up the presentation to a discussion of the proposed solutions. "So, let's open this up for discussion and hear your opinions." For additional ways of obtaining creative ideas, reread the material on creativity and innovation in chapter 4.

Closing—Wrap up

"Thank you so much for all of your good ideas. We'll summarize them in an email and get back to you on our next step."

The Human Side of Gaining Input

Individuals bring a lot of different attitudes to presentations in which they're asked to contribute. Some have strong opinions on the topic; others have little or no opinion and are relatively disengaged. Some individuals love to share their thoughts, while others are reluctant to say much. The role of the presenter is to remember the diversity of the participants and encourage them to contribute by using good human relations.

Keep the following principles from *How to Win Friends and Influence People* in mind when conducting presentations to gain input:

> *Don't criticize, condemn, or complain.*
  Nothing kills participation faster than criticism or ridicule. Participants figure out quickly that the way to avoid condemnation is to keep their mouths shut.

> *Give honest, sincere appreciation.*
  When your listeners hear you give appreciation to another

in the group, they realize that their contributions will be noticed, acknowledged, and valued. This encourages more participation and exchange of ideas and opinions.

> *Make the audience feel important.*
Audience members like to feel that they have valuable, important contributions to make to the discussion. One of the best ways to encourage input is to make everyone feel as though they count, regardless of their position in the hierarchy of the organization.

> *Try honestly to see things from the audience member's point of view.*
Your success at leading this category of presentation will depend to some extent on your ability to convince the listeners that you are open to many different points of view, and that you understand everyone's perspective on the topic.

> *Show respect for each person's opinion. Never say, "You're wrong."*
One of the most challenging aspects of conducting this kind of presentation is the need to keep your own opinions to yourself, and allow people that you disagree with to fully express their viewpoints.

> *Give each person who contributes a fine reputation.*
You have a responsibility in this type of presentation to let every one of your listeners be themselves and express their true viewpoints. Otherwise, you have no need to gain input from the audience. You need to encourage that kind of free exchange of ideas and opinions when you let your listeners know that you respect their good reputation.

How We Sound to Others

Few of us realize how we sound when we speak; we don't hear ourselves as others hear us. An instructor in a public-speaking course asked the students to give a brief introductory talk about something they really know and want to talk about. The students assumed they would get up and breeze along with a fluent and interesting talk. Wrong! The professor taped the talks and played them back. The students were shocked. They never realized how they sounded.

Most of the talks were loaded with what are known as word whiskers—those extra sounds, words, or phrases such as "er," "like," "um," and "y'know," that we use all the time in our conversations. These are very distracting to the audience. Similarly, poor grammar, speaking in clichés, and mispronouncing words will diminish the impact of your presentation. You should tape yourself and listen for filler words and phrases, clichés, and the like, and learn to find "whiskers," just shave them off your speech patterns.

Here are some tips on other common problems that speakers experience, and how to deal with them:

> *Mumbling.–* Mumblers swallow their word endings, making it difficult to figure out what is said. This habit is easily overcome. Don't speak with a half-opened mouth. Open your lips fully when talking. Try practicing this in front of a mirror. It won't take long to correct this problem.

> *Speaking too fast or too slow.–* Many of us have a tendency to race ahead, especially when we're speaking in front of an audience. Whoa! Give people a chance to absorb what you're saying. On the other hand, you may be one of those

slow speakers, who just poke along. The audience will jump ahead, anticipating what they think you are going to say. Keep speaking too slowly, and you'll put them to sleep. You should become aware of your pacing. Practice the talk in front of a friend and get a sense of how quickly you're speaking. Time it. A good pace is between one hundred thirty and one hundred fifty words per minute. And don't forget to slow down when you want to make a point, and speed up to generate excitement.

- *Speaking in a monotone.*– Speaking in a monotone is another sleep inducer. Modulate your voice. Vary volume, pitch, and pace.
- *Standing like a statue.*– Using gestures to emphasize points keeps the audience engaged.
- *Mispronouncing words.*– If you're not sure of a word's pronunciation, look it up. If you're not sure how to say a person's name, ask that person for the correct pronunciation.
- *Failing to observe and react to the audience.*– If you observe that your audience is getting restless, pause, change pace, or introduce an interesting anecdote to get them back.
- *Failing to listen to ourselves.*– As mentioned earlier, we don't hear ourselves as others hear us. Even experienced speakers should tape rehearsals of the presentation or have the actual presentation recorded so that they can evaluate your performance. Once you know your weaknesses as speakers, you can work on correcting them.

Even more effective than a recording is a video of your presentations. You may be surprised how your posture, your gestures, and your overall presence comes across. With this knowledge you can take steps to correct major problems, and tweak less serious missteps, thereby making significant improvements in your presentations.

Sum and Substance

> As you prepare yourself to advance in your career, you should learn how to speak effectively to groups.
> You must learn the step-by-step approach to making presentations so that you can be sure that your messages will be clear, your audience stays engaged, and you cover all the relevant points we wish to make.
> One of the major challenges is making sure that you are not speaking above or below the level of knowledge and expertise of your audience. Make a point to learn as much as possible about the audience before planning the talk.
> In planning the presentation there are five critical elements for success, easily remembered as the "LIONS" formula:
>   - **L**anguage that is easily understood
>   - **I**llustrations and examples
>   - **O**rganize ideas carefully
>   - **N**arrow presentation focus
>   - **S**ummarize
> Structure the Talk
>   - Opening: Statement of topic
>   - State key message: Desired end result
>   - Present key points and expected results
>   - Support with evidence
>   - Close by restating message and reiterating what you want the participants to do.
> Use visual aids to reinforce the message. Charts, graphs, diagrams, and the like can be posted on the walls of the room

or displayed on an easel. Videos could be shown on a small TV screen. Consider creating a Powerpoint presentation that can shown on a large screen.

➤ Statistical tables and charts showing large sets of numbers are best presented as handouts.

➤ Presentations to obtain information take the form of:
- Brainstorming sessions
- Focus groups
- Process analysis meetings
- Problem-solving meetings
- Strategic planning sessions

➤ When seeking to obtain information from the audience members, never criticize a speaker or his or her contribution. Show appreciation for each person and his or her idea.

➤ By taping your rehearsals or actual presentations, you can hear how you come across to the audiences. Listen for poor grammar, word whiskers, clichés, mispronunciations and other errors. Videotaping will show you whether you need to alter your gestures and whether your demeanor is appealing and appropriate.

6

....

ENHANCE YOUR WRITING SKILLS

I n the previous chapter we discussed about how to make oral presentations. However, quite often we are required to put our ideas in writing. Your writing may be in the form of letters sent to customers, vendors, or others; memos or notes sent to your associates, supervisors, or other people in the company; or in the form of email or other electronic media.

Written communication, no matter what form it takes, can play a significant role in how you are perceived by your managers, and it can influence their decisions about your career. As anything you write can be reviewed—even months or years after it was written—it is in a sense a permanent part of your personal brand.

Whether what you write is a letter, memo, or email, you must take special care about how the communication is planned, composed, written, and distributed. In this chapter we will suggest ways of enhancing your writing skills so that anything you write will reflect well upon you.

Preparing the Message

No document or written item you send should be composed without careful preparation. Here are some guidelines to help you minimize missteps and maximize your opportunity to make that message a positive factor in your efforts for advancement.

The Three 'Cs'

Once you've thought out the message, you should begin to formulate the way you'll write it. Keep in mind the three "Cs" of good communication.

Everything we put in writing must be:

Clear— Easy to read and understand.

Complete— Provide all the information we wish to convey.

Concise— Brief and to the point.

For example, if you're writing a memo concerning the status of an order, include the order number, date of the order, identification of materials, and other pertinent information. Be sure to respond to any specific questions. Avoid going into extraneous details that might distract or bore the reader.

The discipline of writing something down is the first step toward making it happen.

Lee Iacocca

Clarity Aids

A goal of good business writing is to be as clear as possible.

Steer clear of complex sentence constructions or extravagant phraseology. Keep your communication as brief as possible. Make your points by:

> Leading with a headline in bold print.
> Write separate sections for each subsidiary point.
> Highlight key points with italics or a different font. If the message is in hard copy, mark key passages with a highlighter. If electronic, use a background color or different color print.
> Use graphs, charts, or other visual aids to augment the impact of our words.

Proofread

What goes out under your name is a reflection of who you are. Even if you have spell-checked your communication, reread it for errors. The spell-check feature in your word-processing program is a great help, as it catches most typos and misspellings, but it is not infallable. A spell-checker will not, for example, let you know that you used "of" instead of "or." A good way to ensure that you do not have errors or omissions in your writing is to read the communication aloud. This technique serves to identify errors that your eyes do not necessarily see.

Writing Need Not Be Formal

In olden times a business letter might read like this: "Pursuant to our telephonic conversation of even date, transmitted herewith are the invoices for the work completed through the ultimate month." Sounds silly, doesn't it? Yes, it was stilted. It's unlikely we would write like that today, but we still are often too formal in our correspondence.

Many of us believe we must be more formal when putting ideas on paper than when communicating them orally, and we use stilted language in letters and business communication.

Such formal language can be perceived as artificial and often insincere. Your message will be clearer and more easily accepted by the reader if you write the way you speak. That sentence would have been much clearer if it had been written this way:

"As I promised when we spoke on the telephone, here are the invoices for the work completed through this month."

On the other hand, the ease and speed with which we can send electronic messages has led to the rise of the opposite writing habit—language that is overly informal. We want to write the way we speak (fluidly and casually) but we don't want our message to sound stilted.

Talk Your Ideas on to Paper

When writing for business purposes, some of us get trapped in web of unnecessary formality. If this is your experience, you can avoid that habit by pretending you are speaking face-to-face or on the phone with the person who will read the communication.

Here are some suggestions for making your writing sound more like you may say it:

Speak your thoughts into writing.– Write with the vocabulary, accents, idioms, and expressions you usually use. You wouldn't normally say, "Please be advised that due to the recent blizzard, your shipment will be delayed until next week." Instead get right into the message: "Because of the blizzard, your order will be shipped next week."

Use contractions. – Instead of writing "You are no longer making that model," or "I cannot attend the meeting," use "We're" or "I can't." Commonly used contractions make your communications read more personally.

Engage the reader. – Oral conversations aren't one-sided. First, one person speaks, then the other comments or asks a question. By interjecting questions or otherwise personalizing the communication, focus the reader's attention on the relevance of your message. For example, instead of writing "We can customize the product to meet your needs," ask "How can we customize this product to meet your special needs?" This compels the reader to reflect how your message is important to him or her.

Personalize the letter. – When we speak we use the pronouns "I," "we," and "you" all the time. But when we write business letters we become more formal. Rather than use pronouns, we tend to write such phrases as "It is assumed...," "It is recommended...," or sentences such as: "An investigation will be made and upon its completion a report will be furnished to your organization." Better to clearly state: "We're investigating the matter, when we obtain the information we'll let you know."

A very effective way of personalizing a letter is to use the addressee's name in the text. If you're friends with the recipient, use the first name; if just business acquaintances, the last name. Instead of writing: "This will result in increased sales," write

"Tim, (or Mr Hunt), this will enable you to increase sales in your territory."

You should give your letters a human touch and do your best to naturally express yourself. Be courteous, polite, and interested. A friendly writing style will please, but a cold one might repel the reader.

Avoid Using Business Clichés

Another way to keep your writing friendly is to avoid using the formal clichés of business communications.

Instead of writing	Write
At a later date	Later (or exact time)
At the present time	Now
Despite the fact	Although
For the period of a year	For a year
In accordance with your request	As requested
In the near future	Soon (or in May)
Is of the opinion that	Believes that
Made an adjustment	Adjusted
The undersigned or the writer	I
We are herewith enclosing	Enclosed is
We are not in a position to	We cannot
With the exception of	Except

Avoid complex sentences

Short sentences (twenty words or fewer) are easiest to read and absorb. Limit each sentence to one idea. It is also helpful to use short, rather than long. Of course, in writing on technical matters to technically trained people, technical language is appropriate. But when writing to people who may not have the technical background, avoid language and jargon that they are unlikely to understand.

> *Reduce your plan to writing. The moment you complete this, you will have definitely given concrete form to the intangible desire.*
>
> *Napoleon Hill*

Making Correspondence Memorable

When we read, the mind processes the words in the same way that it processes words that it hears. You can make your words, (and your business communications) far more effective by augmenting them with visual aids.

Use Graphics

Most people prefer studying a graph or chart over reading a column of figures. By taking a little time to convert information into graphic format, our memos and reports will have much greater impact. If drawings, photographs, or other visual images can be used, the letter or memo comes alive. For people who like to read figures, they can be included as backup data.

There are many computer programs available that can easily convert data into a variety of graph or chart formats. And, if these charts are presented in color, it enhances its impact.

Illustrate Your Message

Where graphics are not applicable, use illustrative stories in our writing. A story enables the reader to picture in his or her mind's eye what we are saying.

Let's look at two memos about labor turnover: "The turnover in the shipping department has caused a heavy workload for the shipping personnel, resulting in accidents, illness due to fatigue, and more resignations. This has led to orders not being shipped and customer complaints."

The above statements are pretty good, but let's see how the information can be related by telling a short story: "I walked into the shipping department this morning. Only six people were working instead of the full staff of ten. They were working under tremendous pressure trying to get the orders out. They had put in ten hours yesterday, and I could see the fatigue in their faces and in the way they worked. One man was limping as a result of a minor accident. While I was there, three customers called complaining about not getting their orders when promised."

The first memo told the facts, but the second example let the reader of that memo "see" the situation. By using visuals and illustrative stories where appropriate, your communications will become clearer and more compelling.

Electronic Communication

By far the greatest innovation in communication in the past few years has been the use of the Internet as a major tool in sending and receiving information.

You must give as much attention to writing emails, text messages, social network messages and other electronic communications as you do to the composition of standard letters and memos. Remember that electronic mail is a form of written communication. It is more than a substitute for a phone call and should not be dashed off with little or no consideration of style or content. Unlike a phone call, electronic messages can be stored and retrieved. They are not "private," and they are admissible as evidence in court. Accordingly, they should be carefully planned and composed.

Better Electronic Messaging

Before composing your message, think carefully about what you want to write. You should plan it as carefully as you would a formal letter. If you are giving instructions, make sure the reader knows exactly what action you're requesting. If you're answering an inquiry, take a moment to carefully read the request to make sure you've gathered all the information necessary to respond appropriately to the questions asked.

Getting the Reader's Attention

Many of us receive dozens, even hundreds, of electronic messages each day. To ensure that your message will be read promptly, use a subject heading that will be meaningful to the addressee. For example, instead of "Re: your email of 6/25," use the subject line or opening to refer to the information provided in that message, for example, "Sales figures for June."As suggested above in composing letters and memos, you should use the three Cs (clear, complete, and concise) in composing emails and messages for other electronic media.

Note that if files are attached to emails, specify in the text which files are attached, so the reader can check to make sure all files have arrived. In media where attachments are not used, specify the file or URL where pertinent documents can be found.

Before clicking "Send," read the message carefully and spell-check it. It's a good idea to read it aloud, which helps us see omissions and other types of errors. Make sure the message is correct in all respects before it is sent.

Email glut can result in your message being ignored or inadvertently deleted. Ask the receiver to acknowledge the message. If the matters involved are very important, follow up with a telephone call to ensure that the message was received and understood.

Privacy Concerns

As we mentioned earlier, there is no assurance of privacy for messages sent electronically. Over and over again we read about hackers who break through highly sophisticated systems. You should assume anything you send electronically can be intercepted. If confidentiality is required, electronic media may not be the best method to use.

Remember that any email sent via the company computer can be read by others in the company. Over the past few years there have been cases in which employees were fired because they sent emails that violated company rules. United States' courts have dismissed their employees' claims of invasion of privacy.

More serious are the cases of employees who have made

comments or jokes in their messages that were considered inappropriate. Any time you use your employer's server, you must assume that the content of your message or search is available to anyone in the company, and ultimately, available to anyone, period. Comments that might be considered sexually or racially inappropriate should never be made. Period. Such messages have been entered as evidence in lawsuits against employees' companies, even though company officials weren't aware of the messages. This has led to termination of the message senders, as well as legal action has been take against both the senders individually and the companies.

Lastly, you should be sure to always look hard at the addressees of your electronic messages. You don't want to "reply all" when your response is only for the individual who sent the original message.

Don't replace phone and personal contacts with electronics. Voice-to-voice or face-to-face contact with people with whom we deal on a regular basis strengthens the personal relationship that is so important in building and maintaining rapport.

Charles Wang,
Former CEO, Computer Associates

Dos and Don'ts for Electronic Messages

1. Do carefully plan messages.
2. Do keep your communications short. If you need to send an elecronic message longer than several paragraphs, warn the recipient at the top of the message and begin with a summary.

3. Do write a descriptive subject line. If you make your readers guess what the message is about, they may rather not read it.

4. Do keep the content and style of the message professional. While informality is find, you'd want to avoid too much punctuation, and the overuse of abbreviations, acronyms, clip art, and complicated formatting. Do not use all caps, as all caps are read as shouting.

5. Do use your spell-checker to assure proper spelling, grammar, and punctuation. After that, proofread the message yourself to assure it is correct in all ways.

6. Do inform recipients when the message doesn't require a reply. It will save both of time and clutter.

7. Do read and re-read your messages before clicking "Send."

8. Do use bullets instead of paragraphs, when this style is appropriate. Bullets often make it easier to read and grasp key points.

9. Do respond promptly to electronic mail received, especially when immediate attention is required. Speed of communication is the chief advantage of this medium.

10. Do use cc: and bcc: sparingly and carefully.

11. Do use the "forward" command sparingly.

12. Do use the "reply" command liberally. It's an easy way to create context for the message.

13. Do indicate whether the message is sent just for the recipient's information or if it requires action or a reply.

14. Do check whether important messages have been received

by asking the respondent to acknowledge it and/or by following-up with a phone call.

15. Do think before we click "send." Sending an email message that isn't well thought out can come back to haunt us. With business correspondence, be careful of exaggerating or being humorous, as our intentions may be misconstrued.

16. Don't forward any message more than two times, as it becomes increasingly hard to follow the stream

17. Don't attach unnecessary files.

18. Don't use electronic mail to replace telephone or personal contacts. It is important to maintain voice-to-voice and face-to-face relationships with the people we deal with.

19. Don't play electronic games, or send or respond to chain letters or similar time-wasters on company time and on company computers.

20. Don't download pornographic material or items that are derogatory to any racial or ethnic groups. Remember that your messages and your searches can be read by anybody and may offend other people in the organization. Engaging in this type of activity could lead to embarrassment and possibly charges of sexual or racial harassment.

21. Don't spread gossip or rumors through electronic media; it's bad enough when gossip is repeated on the telephone or in person, but electronic mail exponentially expands the number of people receiving such information.

22. Don't send a message to your entire list unless the message applies to everyone on it.

23. Don't send off-color jokes or stories on company electronic mail.

Writing Reports that Hit the Mark

Often, one of the important functions of a manager is to submit reports to your bosses or to other managers in the organization. Submitting poorly developed, poorly thought out, and poorly written reports will impede advancement, so it is essential that you put extra effort in preparing and writing these documents.

Let's say your boss has asked you to research and report on a new software package that your company is thinking of purchasing. A good report must contain more than basic information. It should enable the reader to obtain enough knowledge of the subject covered so that he or she can make whatever decisions are needed. As noted for other communications, it should follow the three Cs (clear, complete, and concise).

Research to me is as important or more important than the writing. It is the foundation upon which the book is built.

Leon Uris

Careful Preparation

1. Define the problem or issue that the report will address. Discuss the objective of the report with the manager who gave us the assignment. Much time, effort, and money have been wasted by people compiling reports without knowing what was really wanted. Unless you are entirely clear on how the report will be used, you might spend more time than necessary on secondary aspects of the

situation instead of addressing the really important areas. In this report on new software, your main concerns are three factors: application of the software in telemarketing, cost, and availability of technical service.

2. If you plan to delegate parts of the report to others, break down the project into segments and assign one person to research it. Your job is to coordinate and record the findings and make recommendations.

3. Get the right facts. Assemble all the information needed. For example, for this report your delegatees should speak to the people in the organization who will use the software, and learn what they really want to accomplish by using it. They should obtain literature about the software, read what the technical journals say about it, and speak to people in other organizations who use the product. Information should be sought from the supplier's sales representatives and from representatives from competing software vendors. Get all the information we can.

4. Analyze the facts. Once the information is accumulated, the facts should be correlated and analyzed. One way is to list the advantages and limitations of the software under consideration and make similar lists for other software that also might be viable.

5. Learn the style your readers prefer. The language and form of the report should be tailored to the person or persons who will be reading it. For example, an engineer writing a report for nontechnical managers should try to couch it in language that is as nontechnical as the subject permits. If the use of technical language is essential to the report,

the writer should define and clarify the meaning of the technical terms the first time they are mentioned in the report.

In addition, find out what the reader expects in terms of language, details of content, the use of graphics, and the like. When writing a report for your boss or another manager with whom you have regular dealings, you probably know how to construct the report; if not sure, review reports others have sent for guidance. Some factors to be considered are:

➤ Whether he or she prefers terse, precise reports or a great deal of detail.

➤ Whether that person prefers graphs or charts to statistical tables or likes to see both.

➤ Whether rounded approximations are preferred to exact dollars and cents.

➤ Special information or style the reader uses in his or her reports.

Writing crystallizes thought and thought produces action.

Paul J. Meyer,
Consultant and author

Writing the Report

Although there is no ideal report style, the following guidelines will help structure the report:

State the purpose: A good way to begin is to state the purpose of the report. For example, "As requested in your memo regarding the XYZ software program, here is the information required to make a decision on its practicality for your use."

Summary and recommendations: Although some reports save the summary for the end, many managers prefer reading a summary of your findings and recommendations at the beginning of the report. In this way they can learn the results immediately and read the details when time allows.

Present detailed information: Follow the summary with an organized narrative. Include the details that support the summary and recommendations. Use charts, graphs, and tables if they clarify or reinforce the information in the report.

Watch your language. Keep your language clear and to the point. The variety of fonts and styles now available in most word processing software enable us to present reports in very attractive and interesting formats. Take advantage of this option with an awareness that you want your presentation to look appealing and easy to read. Some people go overboard with display type and other fancy fonts, and these can be both hard to read and can be also overly "cute" for a business report.

Length of report: There is no one ideal length for a business report. It should be long enough to tell the whole story—and not one word longer. Avoid unnecessary duplication—you'll probably want to restate your conclusion at the end of the report, but you should not otherwise set forth the same ideas repeatedly.

Read and reread: Before submitting the report, proofread it carefully. Even a good report loses credibility when it has spelling errors, poor grammatical structure, or sloppy typing. Figures should be checked carefully. Reread it. If possible, have one or more associates read it as well. The make whatever changes are needed, and read it once more to ensure you are satisfied.

Learn how your manager wants to receive the report. Some individuals prefer a hard copy; some an emailed copy that can be downloaded, some both.

Do not send copies to others in the organization unless requested to do so by your boss or the individual for whom you are preparing the report. Unless otherwise ordered, you should keep a copy on our hard drive so you can review it or reproduce it if necessary. Always keep all of the source material used in compiling the report, including material that you researched but did not use in the report. Your research can be valuable when you are asked to expand on what you have written or questioned about facets of the situation you did not include in the report.

Presenting the report orally: There are times when you are asked to give your report orally at a meeting. By following the suggestions on making presentations to inform (see chapter 5) as you write the report, you will be prepared for this contingency.

> *Good sense is both the first principal and the parent source of good writing.*
>
> *Horace*

Sum and Substance

Everything you put in writing must be:

1. Clear—Easy to read and understand.

2. Complete—Provide all the information we wish to convey.

3. Concise—Brief and to the point.

> What goes out under our name is a reflection of us. Reread for errors. Don't rely on the spell-checker to identify all types of mistakes.

> Avoid using overly formal language, which may be perceived as artificial and often insincere. Write the way we speak.

> An effective way of personalizing a letter is to use the addressee's name in the text.

> Memos and reports will have much greater impact if the data is converted into graphic format.

> You must give as much attention to writing emails, text messages, social network messages, and related communications as you do to the composition of standard letters and memos.

> Before composing the message, think carefully about what you write. Plan it as carefully as you would a formal letter. If you are giving instructions, make sure the reader knows just exactly what action you're requesting. If you're answering an inquiry, make sure you've gathered all the information necessary to respond appropriately to the questions asked.

> Review the dos and don'ts for electronic messages. Follow these guidelines and train subordinates to learn and adhere to these rules.

> One of the important functions of a manager is to submit reports to our bosses or to other managers in the

organization. Submitting poorly written reports will impede advancement, so it is essential that you put extra effort in preparing and writing these documents.

➤ Although there is no ideal report style, the following guidelines will help structure the report:

- State the purpose.
- Provide a summary of the conclusion and your recommendations.
- Follow the summary with the details that support the summary and recommendations. Use charts, graphs, and tables.
- The ideal length of our report is the length required to tell the whole story, and no longer.
- Proofread your report before you submit it. Recheck figures and read it once more to ensure you are satisfied.
- Learn the format that your supervisor or the report's recipient prefers, and comply with that preference.
- Manager wants to receive the report.
- Some managers prefer a hard copy; some an emailed copy that can be downloaded on to their computers and some both.
- Always keep all of the source material used in compiling the report, including the material that was not used. Your research can be valuable when you are asked to follow up on your findings.

7

....

ADVANCE WITHIN ONE'S
OWN COMPANY

We can advance in our career by moving ahead in our present company, by changing jobs in our own field, or even by making a complete change in our career. In this chapter we will examine the opportunities in our present organization. In later chapters we will look at when and how to make a move.

Your Present Situation

Your first decision is whether it is best to stay in your present organization or move. Your opportunities are determined by four factors: the industry in which you currently work, your company, your job, and your personal situation.

Your Industry

If your industry has limited growth potential, it will have an impact on your future. Some industries have essentially disappeared because of technological changes; others may have moved out of the area or even the country. For example, Sara's entire career was in the ladies' garment industry, but over time, most of the manufacturing of women's clothing has moved overseas. There is little opportunity in that field. While we cannot predict the future, we must be alert to indicators of change. We must ask:

> Does my industry have a strong history of growth?
> Is my industry in a growth period now?
> Is my industry known for its technological progress?
> Does my industry have a diversified market? (i.e., is it dependent on the government or one particular industry for a high percentage of its sales or supplies?)
> Is the potential market growing?
> Has the number of people employed in my industry increased or decreased in recent years?

Your Company

No matter how good you may be in your profession or occupation, the company for which you work plays a large part in determining your future. If your company prospers, you will advance; if it stagnates your growth will be stymied.

Answer these questions about your company:

> Is the company a leader in its industry?

- Have company sales increased relative to that of the industry?
- Has the company introduced new products or services?
- Has the company kept up with technological changes in the industry?
- Do competitors, customers, and vendors respect the company?
- Is the company's financial basis sound?
- Is the company expanding its personnel?
- Does the company make a practice of promoting from within?
- Is promotion in my company based on merit—not just seniority?
- Is nepotism or favoritism a significant factor in promotion?

Your Job

In every company there are jobs that by their very nature lead to advancement, while others are dead ends. Unless your job is in the former category, you must consider transferring out of it. Answer these questions about the job you currently hold:

- Is your job in the line of promotion?
- Have your predecessors been promoted?
- Is the job a training ground for advancement?
- Does the job give the incumbent opportunity to make decisions?
- Does the job give the incumbent visibility in the company?
- Does it give the incumbent chances to deal with top executives?
- Does the incumbent manage other people?
- Does the incumbent have authority to commit company

resources (money, materials, equipment, work time, and the like)?

❯ Does the job have prestige within the company?
❯ Does the job report to an executive who can recommend advancement?

Personal Situation

Our analysis of our career prospects should also take into account personal factors. We should enjoy our work. No matter what assets a job may have, we're certainly better off if we don't dread going to work every day.

It's worth being candid with ourselves about our present position.

Remain open and objective, evaluate your satisfaction with each of the following items.

❯ Your salary.
❯ The type of work you're doing now.
❯ Your progress in the company.
❯ Your promotional opportunities.
❯ Your supervisor as person to whom you will report.
❯ Your supervisor as a person from whom you can learn.
❯ Your work environment.
❯ The morale of the department's staff members.
❯ The morale of others within the company.
❯ Acquire knowledge and experience that will help you advance.
❯ Acquire knowledge and experience that will improve your professional skills.
❯ Learn things that will make you valuable in your space along with added skill sets that increase your employability.

> The respect you receive from your superiors, colleagues, and subordinates.

> Your next advancement should come in (state desired time). Analyze these items to help you make an objective decision that is not tainted by emotions, grudges, and the like.

Transfer

As a result of this analysis, you may determine that you are stymied in growth in your present position, but that there are many possibilities within your firm for career growth. The answer is not to change jobs but to transfer to another department within the firm.

Intra-company transfers can be accomplished in several ways. Much depends on your relationship with your immediate supervisor. Suppose you have held your position for several years. Your boss is not scheduled to move ahead for quite a while. If you have a good relationship with him or her, you might initiate a friendly talk. Discuss your desire to make more rapid progress than can be attained in your present department, and indicate your desire to transfer to another department where you may be able to advance to achieve your goals more rapidly.

If your boss refuses, or your relationship is such that you cannot discuss transferring with that person, you may decide to talk with a more senior executive—perhaps your supervisor's immediate superior. Request a confidential interview. As that person may have only a cursory knowledge of your background, be prepared to describe your accomplishments as well as your desire to advance. Be sure to express how much you like the company and want to move ahead in it, but because advancement from your present position is inhibited, you desire a transfer. A more senior executive is likely to have the authority to help your desire become a reality. Bear in mind, however, that the executive will probably want to discuss it with the supervisor, who may take issue with your decision to bypass him or her in favor of his or her supervisor. If the transfer is not possible, you may have to live with a diminished relationship with your supervisor. It is a risk you must be prepared to take.

In many companies the ideal way to arrange a transfer is through the Human Resources department. As a rule, the H.R. staff is neutral, and their objective is to utilize all employees to their and the company's best advantage.

The H.R. associate could be approached either informally or more formally. An informal discussion is the more usual approach. You can be assured that your confidence will be honored and your supervisor will not be told of the discussion without your consent. The H.R. associate can give you an impartial evaluation of your standing in the company, where you can go from your present spot, and what lateral moves you are qualified to make. He or she may suggest that you stay where you are for a period of time, recommend that you make a formal application for a transfer, or guide you to areas of activity within the company that you had not considered.

A formal request for transfer may be made either with or without this preliminary informal discussion, although the preliminary discussion is highly recommended. The company may require you to fill out a special form, and in some firms, provide a detailed resume for consideration of the managers of the departments to which you apply. You may also have to be interviewed by some other executives in the company.

If this is the method used in your company, use the same approach that you would use when applying for a job in another firm. (See chapter 9 for more details on interviewing outside your present company.)

Raise in Pay

For many years, raises in many organizations were almost automatic, and one could rely on an annual increment or a merit raise periodically. Sometimes, when a union of blue-collar workers negotiated an increase for its members, supervisory personnel and professional and management staff were given equivalent boosts in pay. We had little or no control over these types of raises. This remains somewhat true today, but in many organizations raises are no longer an expected, regular event. If they are not, or when you desire a special raise, you have to make an overt effort to achieve it.

Traditionally, you will receive a higher compensation when promoted to a more responsible job. Occasionally, you may feel that you deserve a raise when no promotion is imminent. In order to obtain such a raise you must ask for it. The logical person to ask is your immediate supervisor. In most companies this is the only person who can recommend salary increases, although upper level executives in the organization usually must approve them.

Before asking for a raise, learn the wage and salary policy of the company. If there are rigid rules on raises, evaluate how they apply to your situation. In most cases, even rigid rules can be bent under certain circumstances. Where does your current salary stand in the wage range? If you are at the top of the range for your job category, it may not be possible to get a raise under any circumstances unless you are promoted or your job is upgraded. If you are below the top, you can often move up within the range.

Ask for a private interview with your boss. Do not discuss a desire and/or request for a raise with other persons. Your pay increase may cause issues with coworkers that our supervisor does not want to have to address. Never talk to the boss about a raise or promotion at a party or social function. Often promises of raises made when the boss has had a few drinks are "forgotten" the next morning.

In the interview with your supervisor discuss your specific accomplishments. You should not be modest. Point out what you have done above and beyond the basis job requirements and remind him or her of the commendations made on the performance. Anticipate possible objections. For example:

Supervisor: "Business is poorer than last year. Wait until things improve."

You: "I understand, but my production this year is much greater and my contribution to the business should be rewarded."

Supervisor: "You had a raise six months ago."

You: "Yes, and while I appreciate receiving that increase, it was an automatic raise we all received. I feel my work should get special recognition."

Supervisor: "It's against company policy."

You: "I don't want to upset the company, but the wage and

salary policy has some flexibility. I feel that my situation warrants special consideration."

Supervisor: "You are in line for a promotion as soon as a job opens at the next level."

You: "I appreciate that and look forward to it. However, there is no indication that it will appear soon, and I feel that I'm making an exceptional contribution at this time."

Note that you did not request a raise due to your personal need. The case was based on your contribution to the company only. In fact, your personal financial requirements are not the responsibility of your employer, and it is advisable to avoid discussing these issues. Unless you have a strong personal relationship with your boss, the fact that you have had another addition to the family or bought a new house will have little weight in the outcome.

Note also that you did not threaten to quit. Never present an ultimatum to your supervisor. If you "win" you will always be looked upon as a blackmailer; if you lose, you are fired!

Choose the timing carefully. A good time to request an increment is after having received a good appraisal report or after you have done a particularly good job on a tough assignment. It is better to wait than to time your request badly.

The people who get on in this world are the people who get up and look for the circumstances they want, and if they can't find them, make them.

George Bernard Shaw

Promotion

Marian Ruderman, a director at the Center for Creative Leadership in Greensboro, NC, has identified three common myths about promotions:

1. *People get promoted for performance.–* Although performance and accomplishments play a big part, simply being in the right place at the right time is a big factor. In other words, circumstances and opportunity play a large part in who gets promoted. Supervisors often rely on their own intuition and on other people's opinion when deciding whom to promote. They place a big premium on people they trust, and those people that present themselves well. You must always be on the alert to create opportunities for ourselves.

2. *People get promoted because their skills match an opening.–* Although people may get promoted to utilize their specific skills, often a job is created or tailored to fit an employee's abilities. As organizations evolve, jobs are often adapted to match the candidate's skills. You must let your skills be known.

3. *We are competing against several other candidates for a promotion.–* Often the supervisor knows exactly whom he or she wants to promote. If it is you, your job is to convince them that they are making the right decision. If you are not sure, you should increase your visibility and showcase your talents.

Moving Up

The usual route to advancement and more money is via periodic promotion up through the ranks of the organization structure.

The first and obvious step to assure your promotion is to do your job successfully. If you cannot perform at a lower level, you will not usually be considered for higher rank. But superb performance alone is not enough to assure promotion. There are several other factors that go with it.

Early Promotion

Many companies have an almost automatic promotion program at lower levels. A young person joining the company as a management trainee will easily advance to a lower management position within a few years unless he or she is far below standard in performance. Company policy and organizational structure can easily absorb these people.

However, many such promotions may be misleading. They constitute an advancement in rank and initial responsibility, but may lead nowhere.

Career-oriented individuals should choose the type of position desired for their line of advancement, even if it means declining a promotion, which will not further their career.

Ben is an employment interviewer in the Human Resources department of a major manufacturing company. After two years he was offered a promotion to senior interviewer. He asked for a conference with his supervisor to decline the promotion. Ben felt he needed a broader experience in other aspects of human resources management to assure his growth in his profession. The supervisor agreed and withdrew the offer. Six months later, Ben was promoted to an H.R. assistant manager's position at the plant level where he could acquire a variety of experience.

When offered a promotion, you want to think carefully about whether the position is one that you want to pursue. You should ask yourself:

➤ Will this job directly lead to a higher job? Will I gain experience in the job that will make me more valuable to the company?

➤ Will this job give me an opportunity to make decisions? (You can prove ourselves much more rapidly if in a decision-making position. Of course, the risks are higher because a poor decision can have negative consequences.)

➤ Is this job a good temporary step—even if it is not in the direct line of my career goal? For example, working for a short time as an assistant to a senior executive is often a good temporary assignment. You can learn a good deal about many phases of company activity. However, if you have this job too long, you won't acquire real executive experience. You must get out of this position after one or two years and move into a managerial position.

➤ Will this position make me visible to the people who have the power to further my career? No matter how good you may be in your work, if nobody knows about it, you will not move ahead. Some positions are more visible than others. A job that requires frequent contacts with top management has an advantage over the one that does not. The person who thinks first of long-range growth within the company should carefully examine this factor when planning a projected line of advancement in the organization.

In addition to the position you hold and the excellence of your work, two other factors are important to your promotional chances: personal visibility and company politics.

Personal Visibility

In addition to holding a job that provides visibility for you, you should become known to and respected by your company peers and superiors. Once people in the company think of you as a person of repute in your field, you have overcome a basic barrier to advancement—anonymity.

Some rising executives have employed public relations experts to help them achieve maximum visibility, but this is not necessary. Just make sure that your accomplishments become known where they count.

There is no place for false modesty in the struggle for advancement. Let's look at some examples.

When Josh learned that he was not even being considered for the promotion to head his department, he was crushed. His immediate boss for the past five years, Todd, had assured him that, when he retired, he would recommend Josh for the position. Unfortunately, Todd passed away two years before his planned retirement, and the company had hired a new manager from outside the company.

Why didn't the administration consider Josh? Because nobody, other than Todd, knew of Josh's capability. Indeed, none of the upper-level managers even knew Josh. He was "invisible." In most organizations, there are many highly competent people, who, like Josh, will never make much progress because nobody knows who they are. In order to move up in one's career, one must be visible to managers other than just one's immediate supervisor.

How does a person become visible? The first requirement is competence. If you are incompetent and visible, it works against you. Josh was competent, but competence alone is not enough.

When Josh attended meetings with his supervisor, he never contributed his ideas. If he had a comment to make, he jotted it down, and slipped it to his boss, who made the comment. When asked why he didn't present his own ideas, he admitted that he was afraid to speak in front of other people.

Speak Up

One of the most effective ways of becoming known to the executives in your organization is to actively participate in the meetings we attend. Most people who are well rounded in their fields have much to offer. Concern about speaking in public has been identified as one of the most common fears people have.

Yet, it is a fear that can be overcome by training and practice. Courses in public speaking are offered in most colleges and special programs such as the Dale Carnegie Course in Effective Speaking and Human Relations have helped countless people overcome this fear.

Show Interest in Other People's Goals

When Valerie was asked as to what she attributed her relatively rapid rise in her company, she responded: "My big ears." She elucidated: "I really listen to other people—not only when they talk to me, but when they talk to people around me. Early in my career, I was waiting for a meeting to begin and the man next to me was discussing statistical quality control with another person in the group. Some weeks later, I came across an article on this subject in a trade publication. Remembering the discussion, I clipped the article and sent it to the man who had shown interest in it. He expressed his thanks and told another manager how considerate I had been. As that little act meant so much to him, I decided to make a practice of sending copies of articles to various people in the company. I soon developed a reputation of being that thoughtful person who was always looking for information that could be useful to others. This led to my being requested by executives to transfer to their departments and each transfer was an advancement in my career."

Following Valerie's example, you might occasionally send an especially interesting article to a higher executive with whom you have had some contact. Note that it is not wise to contact the president or other senior executives if you do not normally work with them. Stick to the levels immediately above you.

Volunteer

When Bill graduated from college, he joined the Human Resources staff in a large, Fortune-500 company. It didn't take him long to realize that there were at least twenty other bright, young people with whom he would be competing for advancement. He had to do something other than just being an outstanding performer in his job to beat his competition.

Some months later, Bill volunteered to chair the company's annual fund-raising drive for the United Way. In this assignment he visited every department in the headquarters office, and met most of the executives and officers of the company. Each year, for the next three years, Bill chaired the drive.

One of the vice presidents of the company was impressed with Bill's dedication to his assignment and the professionalism with which he handled it. He mentioned a job he wished to create in his department and that Bill might be the right person for it. Bill accepted his offer. Now, instead of being one of many competitors for advancement in the H.R. Department, he became the protégé of a senior executive, with a clear career path ahead of him.

Today knowledge has power. It controls access to opportunity and advancement.

Peter Drucker

Become Active in Professional Associations

Samantha was ready to quit her job in the marketing department of one of America's most prestigious consumer goods companies. She just couldn't see herself moving ahead with so many good people competing with her for advancement.

Rather than giving up, she decided that she had to become visible to the top people in her department so they would recognize her potential.

Samantha was a member of the local chapter of the American Marketing Association. To implement her plan, she agreed to serve on the program committee. Her first assignment was to find a speaker for the April meeting. Her choice was the Vice President of Marketing of her company. Although, she had never spoken to this executive and was certain that he did not even know who she was, Samantha invited him to be the speaker. He not only agreed to address the meeting, but told

Samantha that he considered it an honor to be invited. On two occasions prior to the meeting, he called her to discuss the talk. At the meeting, she sat on the dais next to the speaker and introduced him to the group. From that time on, Samantha was visible to that vice president and began to make excellent progress in the department.

Other means of becoming visible include writing articles for publication in trade journals. If your article involves your activities in the company, get your supervisor's approval before submitting it. This will save you from embarrassment if the work contains any information that is not meant for publication. In most instances your submission will be approved and your status will go up in the company.

You should also consider serving as an officer in a trade or professional association, and participating in community activities in which the company has shown an interest.

Another great way to bring your performance to our supervisor's attention is to have a customer or vendor mention you. If someone with whom you work compliments you, it is permissible to suggest to that person dropping an email or note about your helpfulness or good service to your boss. This type of positive feedback reflects well on your value to your department and the overall organization.

Competence and professionalism are basic to success, but no matter how effective you may be, if the decision-makers do not know you in your organization, you may be overlooked. By planning and implementing a program for your own visibility, your opportunities for career growth should increase significantly.

Visibility is not only a key factor in getting ahead in your current position, but it also serves to expand your opportunities within your industry, your community, and other aspects of your lives. It becomes a helpful tool in obtaining information from other people in the organization, from vendors, customers, and even competitors. I also will enable you to make the most of networking (more on this in Chapter 8).

The Self-Commercial

One excellent way to enhance your visibility is to prepare a self-commercial so that when meeting someone in or outside of the company, you are prepared to provide a clear, concise statement of who you are, what you do, and the unique value that you bring to the business marketplace. It's called a self-commercial because it's so concise and persuasive that people actually listen to you, and remember who you are, and what you can do in terms of results. As any advertising executive could tell you, constructing a statement this creative and succinct is no easy task. The objective is to provide clarity and initiate interest, and do it in less than one hundred fifty well-chosen words (no more than sixty seconds).

Goals of the Self-Commercial

The goal of a self-commercial is to pique the listeners' interest. It should make them curious enough to want to know more. The well-rehearsed, genuine nature of an effective self-commercial creates opportunities for use in limitless settings. Business association meetings, social gatherings, professional groups, and impromptu meetings are all places for potential use.

Creating a Self-Commercial

Let's say you are meeting a senior executive in your organization for the first time. You want to create in impression that he or she will remember favorably. Most likely, sooner or later you will be asked what you do in the organization. Even though you both work in the same organization, do not assume that just stating your job title is enough. Your objective is not to describe the job, but to point out what makes you different, better, and/or more effective than other employees doing similar work.

One way of doing this is to develop a one-minute "pre-cap" of who you are and what you have done. Just as a recap reiterates your story after you've told it, a "pre-cap" is a prologue highlighting what you will later expand upon. This should concisely state your most significant accomplishment on the job.

Example: "I'm an assistant H.R. manager. I love my job because it gives me a chance to be creative. For example, I developed a leadership training program for new team leaders that enabled them to become rapidly productive when assuming their new roles. I did this by designing a series of computer 'games' that covered most of the problems faced by new team leaders, so each trainee could learn at his or her own speed, on his or her own time. We followed this with several interactive exercises and completed the program with a hands-on practice session with an experienced team leader as mentor. This program reduced the training period by 30 percent."

Rehearse the "pre-cap" several times. A good aid is to tape

it and play it back. To make sure that it sounds fresh, don't memorize it. Be prepared to modify it so that you will bring out those factors of your background that is of most interest to the person to whom you are talking. Each time you use it, it should sound original and meaningful to the listener—not like a canned talk.

Company Politics

> *Whenever people work together, be it in a company or a social club, political factors enter into the interpersonal relationships.*
>
> *Erwin Stanton,*
> *Psychologist*

Often there are groups in a company struggling for supremacy. Even in a small firm, there are people competing for advancement and using a variety of tactics to obtain support from other persons in management.

The soundest rule for a new employee to follow is to stay clear of the factional disputes. It is best not to identify with any faction unless and until you are forced to make a choice. It is usually hard to stay away from politics in an organization; eventually all but the most naive people in the management hierarchy will find themselves on one side or another. Often the choice is made for you. You are assigned to a boss and automatically become identified with his or her political group.

If you are on the team that is in the ascendency, it works to your advantage. When your team leader obtains power, you will be rewarded with promotion, and its incumbent benefits.

However, if you are identified with a losing political clique, you may be doomed to a low-level job or forced out.

Choosing sides is a very tough decision. It is best to stay neutral as long as you can. Picking the side most likely to win takes thorough knowledge of the company, its personnel, and the climate in which it operates. By watching the situation closely you may be pulled along with the victors in an in-company struggle. However, if you are associated with the losers, it may be a compelling reason to seek another job.

Most in-company politics are not resolved by a win-lose solution.

They go on with no definite conclusion year in and year out. You can ride along with this by frequent evaluation of where you stand with the in-group and maintaining good relations with all factions. To shift sides is not easy to accomplish without some loss of face, but it has been done, and knowing when and how to do it may assure your survival in the firm.

The Competition

In most firms you will have to compete with persons both in and outside of the department for the jobs above your level. As you go higher in the organization's hierarchy there are naturally fewer positions. The competition for them becomes very keen.

On the way up you must constantly be aware of the rivals for the positions you desire. You should size up your opponents and strive for superior performance and increased visibility.

If you work in a family-owned business, it is possible, if not likely, that only family members will move into top management. In any organization, there may be a competitor who is the boss' favorite or is far ahead of you in the race. In either of these situations, you may find it advantageous to settle for a lower-level plateau in your advancement, or you may choose to learn all you can and then seek a position within the company where there is more opportunity or move to another company. If, however, you feel you can compete, you should do your best to make your mark.

Some of the factors with which you must be concerned are the tactics used by your rivals. Not everyone is going to compete fairly. You may, unfortunately, encounter competitors who will stab you in the back every chance they get, if it will enable them to outshine you.

Although these tactics work with some people, sophisticated executives are aware of them and deplore them. It is the height of poor judgment to belittle one's colleagues. Nonetheless, some of your rivals may attempt to make their way forward by denigrating you and other competitors.

Let us look at some of these tactics and how you can combat them:

> The backbiters: Backbiters will watch every move you make. If you make an error, they will make sure that it is called to the attention of the entire management. They would gloat on every mistake you make. You can combat this by publicizing your accomplishments as discussed above. If you make only the few occasional errors and even the best of us will, your accomplishments will outweigh your errors.

> The negativists: Negativists carefully listen to your ideas and programs. They usually wait until you discuss them at

a meeting with the higher levels of management. Then they strike! They point out all the flaws in the plan and emphasize the negative aspects (e.g., the cost is too high; it's never been tried; it won't be accepted, and the like), even though you have shown how the positive aspects outweigh them. They do not suggest alternatives. The objective is to put you on the defensive and make you look foolish. Unless you are prepared for this, you run the risk of making a poor impression on the other executives. Your plan may be resubmitted at a later time with all the proper answers; but you have lost a significant round. The unfavorable impression they wanted you to make remains in the minds of the senior managers. To repel this type of attack you must always be ready to defend your ideas logically—not emotionally—when they are attacked by negativists. They would love to see you blow up in front of the boss. This would reduce your advancement potential more than most other factors.

> The one-uppers: Unlike the negativists, the one-uppers try to deprecate you by topping any idea you have with one that, at least superficially, outshines yours. For example, you have a well-planned idea for an advertising program that calls for endorsement of your product by a celebrity. The one-uppers hijack your idea by suggesting a specific, very glamorous star. They then direct the discussion to center around "their" star, making it their baby. To combat the one-uppers, put their amendment in its proper perspective. If it has little merit, reiterate the strength of our idea. If it has some value, thank them for contributing to your plan, emphasizing the breadth of possibilities in your idea's execution.

> Sycophants: Every company has its yes-men. Some bosses

surround themselves with sycophants to satisfy their egos. As a matter of fact, knowing when and how to butter-up the boss helps many in furthering their careers. But there is a difference between occasional apple-polishing and sycophancy. Sycophants find excuses to flatter their supervisors. They run to fill every wish; they never disagree and usually parrot their boss' ideas.

Your best approach is to size up your supervisor: if he or she is an insecure person who needs this ego support, you cannot beat the sycophants except by playing their own game. But most executives see through these yes-sayers and are more amused than impressed by them.

You must be true to yourself and hold on to your own ideas. Agree or disagree with your supervisor as warranted and present your disagreements clearly and honestly. Most bosses will usually recognize your right to do this. If they are not convinced that you are right by our arguments, they will respect your right to dissent.

Learn to spot your rivals and to prepare to combat them by analyzing how they operate and by being ready for them.

Good work and recognition of it is still the fastest road to in-company growth. Scheming rivals may cause temporary setbacks, but your integrity will invariably cause you to overcome them.

The Performance Review

One of the most important factors in determining your advancement within a company is the performance review. In most companies, the supervisor usually conducts it annually.

Many of us often fear this meeting. Fear and stress can only work against us in such a critical meeting. With careful planning, you can convert this interview into an asset.

Review Your Own Performance

To get the most out of your performance review, it is essential that you carefully prepare for it. Prior to the meeting with the supervisor, complete an objective review of your performance over the entire period under review. This can be easily accomplished if you have kept a complete log of your activities. If you have not done so, consult all available records.

List Your Accomplishments

From your log, written records, or your memory, identify the major accomplishments over the past year. Include all of the special things you have done that contributed to the success of the department. For example, list the suggestions you made that were implemented such as initiating a safety program that reduced accidents significantly, developing a time-saving method that enabled you to meet a very tight deadline, mentoring a new employee so that she became productive more rapidly, exceeded the quotas for certain work by significant percentages, and similar achievements.

Don't Ignore Your Deficiencies

None of us is perfect. There are some activities in which you know you can do better. Your supervisor is likely to bring this up at the review. Think about the ways in which your performance could be improved, and be prepared to offer methods of doing so.

For example, perhaps you don't know as much as you should about certain technical procedures. It's most likely the boss will comment about this deficiency, so be prepared to discuss what you are now doing to obtain this knowledge.

Your Role in the Review Discussion

Remember the review is a conversation between the supervisor and us. It is not simply an opportunity for your boss to tell you, "This is what you did well; this is what you did poorly." It should be a two-way interaction. True, you may be more of a receiver than a sender in this interaction, but your comments are important.

Listen attentively. – Do not interrupt, but do ask clarifying questions. If what the supervisor is saying is not clear, paraphrase what was just said. Ask, "Do you mean . . .?" or ask a specific question about the statement.

Let the supervisor complete his or her comments before you make any of your own.

Be constructive. – If you do not agree with the boss' comments, you should make a rebuttal. As you have carefully prepared a list of your accomplishments, and are cognizant of your deficiencies, you are ready to make your points.

It's a good idea to start by thanking the supervisor for his or her support over the past year and then say: "I understand everything you have just said and I appreciate your frankness. However, there are certain accomplishments of which I am particularly proud, and for which you complimented me at the time, which you may not have taken into consideration." Then enumerate these items. If deficiencies had been pointed out, do not make excuses for them. Instead, state what you are doing to overcome them. Suggest that your supervisor consider your efforts to improve your performance before the evaluation is made final.

Performance reviews are a two-way street. Both supervisor and subordinate should consider it an opportunity to constructively evaluate the performance and develop plans for continuous improvement.

Scott Ventrella,
Consultant and Author

Set Goals for the Future

In many organizations, the performance review period is a time for setting goals for the next period. Discuss how close you came to reaching the goals set at the previous review. If during the year these goals had not been met, explain the circumstances.

Discuss what your goals are for the ensuing period. These may be in the form of specific job-related objectives such as increasing production or developing new projects, or business-related personal goals such as learning a new language or computer program or working toward a college or graduate degree. Make sure that these goals are important to the company and will enhance our opportunities for advancement. Point out that you are committed to accomplishing them.

If you follow these suggestions, you can make your performance reviews work for you and become a valuable stepping-stone to your career advancement.

Sum and Substance

➤ Analyze your opportunities by studying the situation of your industry, company, and present job, as well as your personal goals.

➤ If you are satisfied with your company, but your job does not offer opportunity for advancement, consider a transfer to another job in the organization.

➤ If promotion or transfer is not an option, follow the suggestions made in this chapter to obtain a raise in salary.

➤ To enhance your opportunities for promotion:

  • Become an expert at your job and take advantage of opportunities to showcase your talents, create a product, fix a problem, and/or get results.

  • Demonstrate excellent communication, leadership, and presentation skills.

  • Exceed expectations. Do more than promised, come in under budget, and beat deadlines.

  • Show a genuine desire to learn. Ask questions, be a good listener, and show an interest in others, and how their job relates to yours.

  • Demonstrate a steep and impressive learning curve.

  • Know the boss's priorities and contribute to those projects.

  • Take advantage of and seek out training opportunities.

  • Stay away from politics and gossip.

  • Learn to deal effectively with a diverse population.

  • Do the homework. Research the position or promotion you are seeking. Let your aspirations be known.

  • Speak up in company meetings—but be sure what you say is pertinent and correct.

- If we have made a noteworthy contribution to the job, take credit for it (and be sure to give credit to those who assisted you.) It is not necessary to exaggerate or to denigrate others to gain this recognition.
- Read trade and technical journals. Clip or forward articles you think your supervisor would find of interest. Occasionally send an especially interesting article to a higher executive with whom you have had some contact.
- Attend and take notes at professional and trade association meetings and report matters of interest to your bosses.
- Write articles for trade publications. If they involve your activities in the company, get the supervisor's approval before submitting them.
- Innovate. Make suggestions on improvement on products and/or service. But be sure that your suggestions have relevance to the company's goals. Weak suggestions made just for the sake of getting you noticed will backfire.
- Become active in a professional or trade association. Volunteer to read a paper or arrange and chair a meeting. Invite or supervisor to attend or even participate in the program.
- Ask the boss for advice and counsel regarding your growth prospects. Ask for suggestions on courses you can take or books you should read.
- If a customer, vendor, or other outsider praises your work, ask that person to write a note to your boss. Obviously you do not solicit this type of endorsement, but if the same customer praises you frequently, an off-hand remark such as, "I'm glad my suggestion helped you

solve that headache. Ron would find it useful if you told him about it," is not out of line.

- Do something over and beyond the call of duty. Make sure it is something that gets publicity in the company. Head up a company charity drive; take an assignment nobody else wants; write articles for the company newsletter, etc. Get your name known in a favorable way throughout the firm.
- Prepare for performance reviews by listing your accomplishments over the year and indicating what you are doing to overcome your deficiencies.
- Be patient. Promotions don't happen overnight.

When one door closes, another opens: but we often look so long and so regretfully upon the closed door that we do not see the one which has opened for us.

Benjamin Disraeli

8

....

SEEK A NEW JOB—SOURCES OF
JOB LEADS

W e may be seeking a new job involuntarily because we have lost our current job. In today's economy, layoffs are common, and you must be prepared to look elsewhere for work if your organization restructures its staffing and lets you go.

On the other hand, after evaluating your current situation and studying the results of your assessment (suggested in chapter 7), you may decide that opportunity in your current company is limited and accordingly look for a new job in another organization. Caution! Changing jobs voluntarily is a serious matter and a decision to change jobs should not be made lightly. Before you begin a search for a new position, you should consider the following:

- Review your evaluation of your position and the organization and be sure that there is sufficient reason to leave the company.
- Never change jobs for purely emotional reasons. If you are quitting because you do not like the supervisor, be sure that this dislike is so overpowering, it outweighs the advantages the company offers. A transfer to another department may be a better choice.
- Never quit or threaten to quit because of a disagreement. Stay on the job until a new one is obtained. Being employed will obviously alleviate the financial and emotional strain of unemployment, but it is also preferred by many companies to hire people who are currently employed.

> *The secret of getting ahead is getting started. The secret of getting started is breaking your complex overwhelming tasks into small manageable tasks, and then starting on the first one.*
>
> *Mark Twain*

Planning the Job Search

Seeking a job is a major undertaking and must be carefully planned. It cannot be done haphazardly. Consider it a sales campaign in which the product being sold is your ability to be of value to the potential employer. The plan includes:

- A careful analysis of your background—what you offer that employer.
- Developing a list of sources of job leads.

> Writing a résumé that sells.
> Preparing for interviews.

In this chapter we will discuss the first two items. The latter two will be covered in Chapter 9.

Your Personal Accomplishment Inventory

The first step in your job search is to review your entire background and compile an inventory of your accomplishments. Here are some of the things you should indicate:

Education

If you are not a college graduate, note all education or training that is pertinent to the position sought.

If you are a college grad, identify college, degree(s) and any special accomplishments or honors. If you've been out of college for five years or less expand on this, if you've been out of college longer than that, education becomes less important than work experience, so there is no need to detail your academic experience.

In either case, specify any specific programs taken that show you are keeping up with the state of the art in your field. Indicate certifications and licenses such as CPA, PE, member of state bar, and the like.)

Note memberships in professional, occupational, or industry associations. If pertinent, list publications in which your work has appeared, participation in industry conventions, etc.

Work Experience

List each job held starting with your present or most recent position, and work backward. It is your most recent experience that is most likely to incorporate your experience that is closest needed for the position sought. For each job:

List name and address of the organization, dates of employment, and title of your position. If you have held a variety of positions in the same organization, treat each position as a separate job. Indicate starting and last or current salary, the name of supervisor and your reason for leaving.

Note: Don't use all of this information in your résumé (see chapter 9), but you will need it for company application forms and often at the interview.

In preparing answers to questions that might be asked, list specific problems that you faced and how you dealt with them. These solutions will provide evidence of your accomplishments.

By developing a personal accomplishment inventory, you will be well on your way to writing your résumé, discussing your backgrounds with people in the network, and responding to questions likely to be asked at interviews.

The average person puts only 25 percent of his energy and ability into his work. The world takes off its hat to those who put in more than 50 percent of their capacity, and stands on its head for those few who devote 100 percent.

Andrew Carnegie

Sources of Job Leads

There are a great many ways to become apprised of work opportunities. You'll have to be open-minded in your job search, as you never know how you might find your next position.

Using Internet Referral Services

Internet referral services are the online equivalent of newspaper job listings. There are two ways that job seekers can use these services. One is to search the listings for job openings; the other is to place our résumé in their data bank. Applicants are not charged a fee for either service.

There are many Internet referral services currently online, and many more seem to appear every month.

Most services charge a fee to companies to list their jobs. There is no charge to applicants. Once an applicant registers with the service, he or she can search their files, post their own résumés, and get tips on writing a résumé, and in using the service. Among the most prominent of these are Career Builders (www.careerbuilder.com), Monster (www.monster.com), and Indeed (www.indeed.com). Job postings also appear on Craigslist, and there are job sites specializing is specific industries and professions.

Searching Job Listings

Even if a company has its own website, it can't depend on the job applicant best suited for that job to log onto its site. To cast a broad net, companies place ads on one or several of the Internet referral services. These ads are far more comprehensive than most newspaper ads—you can learn much more about the position from them. By using key words you can select appropriate listings, and if interested, make direct contact with the employer.

Placing Your Résumé with the Service

A very effective way of finding a job is to place your own résumé in the job bank. Just as you scan the job listings, employers scan the applicant file to seek people for their jobs.

Remember that the only way our résumé will come to the attention of the employer is the result of a search. Just as the company used key words to attract applicants to its listings, you have to use key words that employers will search and that will point out your qualifications for the job. Job titles are okay, but they are often too general or company-specific. They may also result in so many hits that your gets lost. Use a specific title, not a general one. If you list "manager," your résumé will be mixed with managers in all sorts of categories. Use the title that best describes you: "production control manager," or "men's clothing store manager," or "training and development manager."

When placing your résumé in an employment database, you need not necessarily use a job title. Because jobs are not placed alphabetically by title (as they are in newspaper classified ads), but are accessed by key word, select a word or phrase that companies are likely to consider as descriptive of the job they are seeking to fill. Instead of writing "computer scientist," use a more specific phrase such as "software designer," or "financial systems analyst."

Include key words that amplify your experience in the

résumé, such as "designed and developed," or terms that indicate special knowledge. A computer expert might list the names of programs or systems used; a human resources manager might indicate major areas of experience such as "union negotiations," or "executive development." A sales executive might highlight the markets covered, such as "major food chains" or "industrial manufacturers."

Once a company selects our résumé, it will contact you by mail, phone, or letter. Often the company representative will ask for more information and/or conduct a telephone interview with you before deciding whether to invite you in. Before responding to an inquiry, log on to the company's website and get as much information about the company as you can. This will prepare you to present yourself more effectively when you do make the contact.

The job market is supply and demand. You're the product and there are tons of you. Adjust accordingly.

Megan Pittsley,
Career Coach

Answering Want Ads

Another source for seeking a job is in the help-wanted ads that are placed in newspapers and magazines. As with positions posted on the Internet, because of the tremendous number of responses ads generate, your chance of getting the job you want from an ad is relatively slim. However, it does pay to read these ads and respond to those in which the requirements are close to your background.

Every large city and many smaller communities have at least one newspaper that carries want ads. In addition, many papers print larger ads (called display ads) for executive and technical positions, usually printed on the financial or business pages.

Ads in local or major city papers are only one source for job openings. There are also trade publications in every industry, occupation, and profession that carry help-wanted advertisements. For example, executives and administrative personnel will find the *Wall Street Journal* an excellent source of job openings.

Like with job postings on the web, many print ads do not identify the company seeking to hire. Instead, company identification is by means of a box number. Companies use these "blind ads" for a number of reasons. For one, they do not wish to let their own staff know they are thinking of replacing somebody. They also may not want to be flooded with applicants directly calling them. In addition, they may want to avoid the awkwardness of being pressed by friends, relatives, customers, and others to consider and interview unqualified applicants.

If you're unemployed or are openly seeking a position, there is no problem involved in answering a blind ad. However, if you are currently employed you should exert great care in answering an ad because it could very well be your own company that is advertising.

The best advice is to refrain from answering any blind ad where the description sounds very similar to that of your current employer.

Obviously, if the ad says the position is in the rubber industry and you are with a brewery, there is no danger. If there are no means of identifying at least the general area in which the company operates, it is wise not to respond to that ad.

If the position description identifies the company, you are relieved of this type of doubt. Generally, a company will "sign" an ad when it wishes to attract people who know the company's reputation and when they want candidates to answer without fear that it may be their own firm.

In answering any ad (blind or signed), be sure to read the text carefully. Determine what it is that the company is seeking. Is there something particular in your background that is especially pertinent to what they want? If your résumé does not highlight these factors, supplement what's on the résumé with a cover letter pointing out your background in the areas sought by the employer.

Keep your cover letters brief, and tailor the letter to fit the requirements of the job, matching them point by point. This is particularly helpful when the ad is very specific as to the company's requirements. The enclosed résumé will give the rest of the story.

Using Employment Agencies

To use an employment agency effectively, it is helpful to understand how they work and what we can do to get the best results through their efforts.

One of the first things to be determined about an agency is whether it handles the kind of positions in which you are interested. It is seldom profitable to file an application with an agency that rarely or never advertises positions in your field and/or your particular salary range.

When you find an agency that shows promise, visit it and ascertain whether the staff members there really understand your needs and have the expertise and contacts to best work on your behalf. At the agency, you will be assigned to a counselor. This person should be familiar with the employment market and should give you a good deal of information about current possibilities in your field. He or she should review your résumé and make suggestions as to how it can be improved (be prepared for this.) If there is a specific position for which you may qualify, the counselor can suggest how your résumé can be tailored to emphasize those aspects of your background that would be of most value to that employer.

To get the most benefit from an employment agency:

> Be entirely frank with the counselor in discussing your objectives.

> Make sure to obtain his or her evaluation of your marketability.

> Keep in mind that agency staff members have an intimate knowledge of salary ranges and benefits, and usually have this data for other geographic areas besides the one you are in.

> Keep in touch with the counselor at agreed-upon intervals, so that he or she is certain of your continued interest and availability.

> When you are referred to a prospective employer, keep the

agency closely informed of your progress. This is particularly essential in a situation where a number of interviews are scheduled before the company is ready to make an offer. In such cases, the agency—by being in touch with both you and the prospective employer—is able to give additional advice and information between the interviews that can often be very valuable.

How many agencies should you work with? It is not wise to limit ourselves to only one, nor should we indiscriminately send our résumé to every agency in our city. It is a good idea to read the employment agency advertisements for your own city, as well as for those areas in which you might wish to relocate. Even if there is no specific listing that fits your needs, if the employment agencies have opportunities in your general area of interest, it pays to contact them.

Very often, potential employers, business friends, and personnel executives (within companies that deal with agencies) can suggest good agencies to contact. Get the best advice you can on which agencies are the hardest working and the most effective. This will save you time!

The same suggestions that apply to private employment services also work well when making your availability known to technical and professional societies, college alumni placement offices, and other organizations that may refer employment seekers.

Executive Recruiters

If you are seeking a position with a salary over $100,000 per year, executive recruiters are another good resource.

These professionals differ from employment agencies in that they work exclusively for employers and tend to work with individuals in specific fields or industries. Executive recruiters rarely advertise their openings. Typically, they research a field to identify suitable candidates and then approach them directly. Most of the people hired through this technique are currently employed and may not even be thinking about changing careers or positions when contacted. Recruiters do not work to help an applicant seek employment. Indeed, this would defeat their purpose.

One of the best and easiest sources for recruiters to tap is their own files. So, it is advisable to send a résumé to those recruiters who work in your areas of interest. Write a brief letter outlining your salary requirements, willingness to relocate, and other pertinent data. Some recruiters may invite you for an interview. However, the great percentage of recruiters will just file the letter for future use. Today it's most likely that you'll be asked to file your résumé with them electronically. If and when your file pops up in a search, they will contact you.

A telephone call to the executive recruiter is probably a waste of time. The only exception to this general rule would be if the recruiter is willing to see you as a courtesy to a mutual colleague or a company such as your former employer. Such an interview may slightly increase your chances of being considered for one of their current or future searches. Most firms today have a centralized file where the notations of all the associates are located. If a recruiter actually meets you and thinks you are a good candidate, it will be noted on your file, and you will be bumped up to a higher priority category. A directory of executive recruiters can be purchased from:

Kennedy Career Services

1 Phoenix Mill Lane, 3rd Fl.

Peterborough, NH 03458 USA

Phone: 800-531-0007 or 603-924-1006

Fax: 603-924-4460

Customer Support: customerservice@kenn edycareerservices. com

Many libraries and virtually all business libraries have a copy of this comprehensive directory. It is worth spending a few hours looking through the thousands of listings, which are broken down by function, industry, and geography.

> *The person who goes farthest is generally the one who is willing to do and dare. The sure-thing boat never gets far from the shore.*
>
> *Dale Carnegie*

Employment Counseling Services

Don't confuse employment-counseling services with executive recruiters. If you do, this is no accident, as their ads give the impression that they are recruiters. However, these types of organizations differ considerably. For one, employment-counseling services charge a fee to the employment-seeker. For that fee, they provide guidance on how to proceed on one's employment search. These services may include an evaluation of one's educational and work background, writing a professionally done résumé, preparing direct mail campaigns, and many other things. There is no assurance that their participation in our search will lead to a real placement. They can offer no promises for our money. Their fees vary from several hundred dollars to several thousand dollars depending on what services you buy. Most of what they offer you can do yourself by following the guidelines mentioned in this book.

Outplacement Services

In addition to serving individuals looking for work on their own, employment counselors are also by employers to assist employees who are laid off in finding a new job. As the company pays their fees, the applicant should take advantage of these services. They can be most helpful in getting you started on the right track in your job search, but there is no guarantee they will succeed, so you must be ready to also use the other sources discussed in this section.

> *To get ahead—and get hired—you have to get through some grunt work. If you can break complex undertakings into smaller ones, you can get started—and get done— faster.*
>
> *Kevin Donlin,*
> *Minneapolis Star Tribune*

Using the Internet for Job Leads

The company that may hire you will most likely use online searches and research to identify qualified candidates for their job openings.

Using Company Web Pages

As a job seeker, the Internet has made it easy (and therefore even more necessary) to research companies we may be interested in working for. It is a must to visit the company website, in addition to doing a broad Internet search to see what positive or negative statements have been made about it. You should take significant time to become familiar with all of their products or services, and of course the types of jobs they provide, and their listings of current job openings.

A survey of one thousand corporate recruiters found that most reported spending a significant part of their recruitment budget on the Internet, and this is growing exponentially. Many companies have special websites dedicated to job openings. You can reach them by logging on to the company's principal website and clicking on the link of job listings.

Most companies provide substantial information about its business and opportunities on its website. Unlike advertising in a newspaper, the listing is not competing side by side with ads from other companies and is not limited by the space and format requirements of print ads. This allows you to study what the company offers and what the job requires. If it fits your background and job objectives, you can make immediate contact via email or telephone. In addition, you can prepare a special résumé that will emphasize those aspects of your background that fits the job requirements. (More on how to do this will be found in the discussion of résumés and letters in Chapter 9).

Even if there are no immediate openings, you can enter the pertinent information in your resource file for future reference.

Using Social Media

In the past decade, social networking sites have become an integral part of our daily lives. As a result, it is imperative for all job seekers to utilize social media as a tool to help expand their professional networks and identify potential career opportunities. The most effective social networks for career-seekers are Facebook, LinkedIn, and Twitter.

If you are on Facebook, think of how many friends you may have. Fifty? One hundred? Five hundred? Now, think of how many friends each one of your friends has. Simple arithmetic will reveal that you are within two degrees of separation from thousands of individuals. Though you may classify these individuals as "friends," each one of them can be a helpful member of your professional network. Start by reviewing your friends on Facebook and the connections they may have—one might have a family member in your trade or have a friend that works at the company where you are applying for a job. A simple, sincere Facebook message to this individual asking him or her to reconnect, and eventually requesting assistance in your job search may lead to a direct referral for that position, and help get your résumé to the top of the pack for review.

While Facebook is often your personal online home, LinkedIn can be considered your professional one. If you aren't yet on LinkedIn, sign up today and create an online profile. This is particularly important if you are beginning or in the midst of a job search. Your LinkedIn profile is essentially your online professional résumé, one that potential employers can connect to at their convenience (You should also include the link to your LinkedIn profile on your print résumé.) Once your profile is set up, you can begin making connections with those you have worked or gone to school with in the past. By creating a group of connections, the service itself will then automatically suggest new ones. Each connection must be justified so you know they are meaningful. Pretty soon, you will notice that you are closely connected to hundreds, if not thousands of individuals in your field, and you can identify which organizations they work at and who else works there. Many employers are also listing jobs on LinkedIn, through the jobs section or their organization's own LinkedIn page, complete with a news feed, discussion board, and analytics on the company's employees, which are great resources for research.

Twitter is also an important social media tool. Consider Twitter a microblog, or your personal newsfeed. Your newsfeed consists of the one hundred forty characters-or-fewer updates of the people or groups you are following. Once you start tweeting, people will follow you. If you use Twitter professionally, people in your field will notice what you are saying, and you can keep abreast of issues in your professional field, including links to job openings and other professional development opportunities. A key function of Twitter is the hashtag #. If you are interested in marketing news, search under the hashtag #marketing, and you will see updates of what is trending in the field. You can do the same for #marketingjobs, #educationjobs, #engineeringjobs and so forth.

Utilizing social media is just one part of your career-search strategy. Career development is an ongoing process of marketing your skills and abilities, making meaningful connections, and identifying career opportunities strategically. It's best to frequently evaluate and reflect on your process so that you can shift it as needed. As fast as the work world goes these dynamic times, effective use of social media will help you keep and stay ahead, positioning you for career success.

Caution: While we may limit the people who can view our Facebook page and the like, it's best to simply expect that anyone can access anything we post on a social media site. Be careful to never write or post something you would not want a potential employer to see.

Networking—Uncovering the Hidden Job Market

The slave has but one master, the ambitious man has as many as there are persons whose aid may contribute to the advancement of his fortunes.

Jean de la Bruyère,
French Essayist

Most of the desirable jobs are not even known to agencies or recruiters. Recruiters typically handle only about a relatively small percentage of the total number of jobs filled in any given year. Most positions are filled by word-of-mouth. Sometimes a company is not actively seeking candidates, but expresses interest in seeing people who might fit its current or prospective needs. Some companies may be planning expansion or reorganization, and although they are not actively searching, will interview and hire qualified people who are brought to their attention. In some cases if a company finds someone who really impresses them, they may even create or change an existing job to attract that person into the company.

When an employer has a particularly desirable job to fill, it is likely to try to fill it the same way you would try to find a good dentist, auto mechanic, or lawyer; you would ask your friends and colleagues for recommendations.

By building up a network of people who can recommend or direct us, we can create a resource that nobody else has. The value of networking is that its reach is unlimited. Each person on our list is a source for additional people to contact. As our list grows, so do our chances for finding a position through this invaluable resource. Often, networking uncovers a position that we would otherwise have no way of knowing about.

Growing Your Network

There are several sources for building up your network. If you wish to limit your search to a specific market, you may choose to concentrate on the industry in which you are interested. If you wish to stay or locate to a particular location, you develop a network in that area. If you are more flexible, you have wider choices.

Some sources to explore are:

> Friends.– Many of our social friends and acquaintances have contacts that may be helpful in our search, even if they are not in any way connected with the industry in which we are interested. For example, your dentist or doctor may have patients in the area in which you are seeking employment who would be assets in your network.

> Business associates.– Over the years you have met many men

and women in your business activities. These include sales reps who call on many companies that may have jobs in our field, competitors, customers, vendors, service technicians, and the like. Of course, if you are currently employed, you must be sure not to jeopardize your position by expressing your desire for a new one.

> Newspapers.– Read the business section of the newspaper. Often articles in the paper provide the names and companies of people who could be leads or provide leads for jobs.

> Business journals.– Trade journals and newsletters in your fields of interest are excellent sources of names and contact information for potential employers.

> Trade and professional associations.– If you are members of pertinent associations, you can draw on their membership rosters for your network lists.

> Alumni associations.– Graduates of your schools will often make special efforts to help often.

> Nonprofit organizations.– Community groups, religious groups, charities, and other nonprofit organizations are good places to make contacts for your networks.

> Social media.– As discussed earlier in this chapter, Facebook, LinkedIn, Twitter, and similar Internet networks are designed for networking.

Everyone is potentially a contact either now or in the future, so burn no bridges behind you.

Susan B. Joyce,
Career coach

Managing on Network Contact File

It is never too early or too late to start a networking file. Many young career-oriented men and women start while still in college. If you haven't started one, yet, begin immediately. The networking file can take many forms. Among them are:

› Computer programs.– Countless computer programs are available with which we can make our network files easy to access. If you use a Mac, you can use the Address Book application that comes with your computer. Because the majority of your networking will be done online, it's easiest for most of us to have our network files on our hard drive. However, there are other methods that work just fine, and we'll look at them below.

› Business cards.– Saving business cards is an easy approach, but it can be a little unwieldy. Whenever possible, keep business cards systematically filed. The obvious advantage to saving business cards is that the name of the person, his or her title or position, company name and address, phone number, and email address are neatly provided for us. On the back of the card write any other pertinent data, such as any circumstances that will help to remember that person. Be aware that today, special scanners are available that can scan business cards right into your computer.

› Rolodex or similar system.– Some business executives consider this type of system essential to doing business, and place all of their business contacts in these types of files. A special Rolodex or card file can be developed for your network, alongside the one used in normal business dealings. The information would be similar to that recommended for the business card file, but you might find this method even more convenient.

➤ Cross-Index file.– The chief problem with business card or Rolodex systems is that they are usually filed alphabetically. A cross-index card system enables us to categorize our contacts and locate people accordingly. Several computer programs are available to sort and classify our lists.

Using Your Network

Let's see how networking might actually unfold. Jane Ross, the human resources manager at the Dimple Doll Company was asked to give a talk at a meeting of the FOBs (Family-Owned Businesspersons)—an organization of young men and women who work in businesses owned or dominated by their family. She sat next to Scott Rice at the luncheon that preceded her talk.

Scott Rice is the Vice President of manufacturing for Fibre-Mold, Inc., a custom plastics molding firm. Jane learned that his company was a major producer of ballpoint pen casings. Immediately after the meeting she made up a card for him (as well as for the others she had met). He was cross-indexed under "plastics" and "company owners." His index card or computer-based file would look like this:

Basic information:

Category: Plastics

Company owners

Name: Rice, Scott

Title: VP – Mfg.

Company: Fiber-Mold, Inc.

Address: 24 Dove Place, Farmingdale, NY 11404

Phone: 631-777-9876

How Known Met at FOB meeting, January 20, 2012

Comments: Co. manufactures ballpoint pen casings. Father founded company and is still active. Scott is slated to move up when his father retires in a few years. He runs manufacturing operation, discusses problems of converting to team management is active in plastics trade association, Long Island Chamber of Commerce, and local chapter of Sierra Club.

He is married and has 3 children. He is a deep-sea fisherman and he also likes camping with his children.

Any other contacts or further information can be added to the file. Jane had no reason to call Scott until a year later when she had to make a career move. When she called, she reminded him of the previous meeting.

Jane: "Scott, this is Jane Rose of Dimple Dolls. We met a year ago in January, when I gave a talk on supervisory techniques to the FOBs."

Scott: "I certainly remember you. I used several of your ideas and they have worked great."

Jane: "Glad they were of value. Do any fishing lately?"

Scott: "Just came back from three days off Montauk Point. Caught some tuna and sailfish. Nice of you to ask. Now, what can I do for you?"

Jane: "Dimple Dolls has been acquired by Giant Toys. The H.R. function will be handled by Giant, and my job has been eliminated. I would appreciate the opportunity to meet with you to discuss my career opportunities."

They arranged to meet the following week. Although Scott did not have a job for Jane, he made several useful suggestions to improve her résumé. She thanked him for the interview and asked, "Do you know anybody who might be able to help me in my job search?" Always ask this question after all networking interviews. This is the way to expand your contacts and build your network.

Scott referred Jane to Bill Vance, the owner of a large trucking company. He said "Bill probably will not have a job in your field, but his company services dozens of manufacturers in this area, and he may know of someone who'd have an opportunity for you."

The Follow-Up Note

Good networkers *follow every contact*—whether it produces a lead or not—with a thank-you note. If the connection was made over the telephone, and you did not give the individual a résumé, you can attach one to your thank-you letter. A mailed note or letter is considered a nice touch, but most of the time an emailed thank-you letter is adequate. Jane wrote:

Dear Scott,

Thank you for the time you gave me out of your busy schedule when we met on Tuesday. I am most grateful for the lead to Bill Vance. I called him and learned that he was out of town until next week. I'll call again then.

I made the changes you suggested to my résumé; enclosed is a copy.

Any further ideas you have for me will be sincerely appreciated.

Sincerely,

Jane R. Ross

Jane then entered the following information in Scott's file:

8/6/11: Called to ask for appointment to discuss career opportunities.

8/8/11: Met with him. Received good advice and lead to Bill Vance of Vance Truckers.

8/9/11: Sent thank-you note.

8/9/11: Phoned Bill Vance, out of town, back 8/16.

Networking is not limited to employment searches. You can use it for any business inquiry, such as seeking referrals when you are looking for personnel, checking references, and/or any type of situation where others may freely give you the information you need. Networking is invaluable, and it's serious business, worthy of your strictest attention and valuable time.

It is critical to keep a record of each contact. You may not call a person on the list for months or even years, but if you make a contact after a long period, referring to your last discussion or even your first meeting can melt the ice and help establish rapport.

Some of the best sources for your network files are people who, by the nature of their work, have many contacts. For example, pay special attention to officers of trade and professional associations, editors of trade publications, bankers in your community, political leaders, and the like. These people are centers of influence. Mark their files with a star. They people should be among the first people you approach when you have to.

Sum and Substance

- Changing jobs voluntarily is a serious matter and should not be done lightly.
- Consider the job search a sales campaign in which the product being sold is your ability to be of value to the potential employer.
- The first step in your job search is to review your entire background and compile an inventory of your accomplishments. This will be the source for your résumé, discussing your backgrounds with people in your network, and responding to questions likely to be asked at interviews.
- In listing the work experience in each job, include:
  - Basic duties
  - Responsibility in managing people (number, job categories, level in management hierarchy, coordination as team, hiring and firing, etc.)
  - Responsibility for managing money, materials, methods, or other special activities.
  - Major accomplishments on the job. Indicate results in terms of money saved, increased profits, time saved, markets expanded, etc.
  - What you liked most about this job. Why?
  - What you liked least about this job. Why? (This information is for your own purposes of reflection. It is not advisable to tell others negative things about your former employer or about your experiences working for

your former employer.)

> The sources you should use may include:
  - Internet job sites
  - Newspaper and trade magazine want ads
  - Employment agencies
  - Executive recruiters
  - Employment counselors
  - Social media
> Networking

By building up a network of people who can help us, we can create an individualized resource. The value of networking is that it has unlimited potential.

It is never too early or too late to start a networking file.

After meeting or conversing with a networking contact, always send a thank-you letter. The letter shows your professionalism, gives you a chance to recap the discussion, and an opportunity to send a résumé to the individual if he or she does not have one.

9

SEEK A NEW JOB—THE RÉSUMÉ
AND THE INTERVIEW

The key components in your search for a new job are:

1. Your résumé.
2. The job interview.

Your Résumé

Your résumé is one of the essential elements of your career search. It is usually the first contact that you have with a prospective employer. If the employer is not impressed with your résumé, you will probably not get the chance to meet him or her and personally present your qualifications, and *sell ourselves*!

The résumé is a summary statement of your education, experience, and general background that is offered to prospective employers. It is used when answering an employment ad, is sent to employment agencies and/or recruiters, or as a networking tool.

The résumé is your advertising piece. It should stress your strengths and minimize your limitations. Unless something on that piece of paper excites the reader, that all-important interview will never take place.

You've got to accentuate the positive,
Eliminate the negative
And latch on to the affirmative.

Johnny Mercer

Preparing to Write Your Résumé

Before writing your résumé, you should carefully review your entire background with emphasis on your accomplishments thus far in your career.

Just writing a job description of your position is not enough. Most of your competitors must have similar experience. You must play up your accomplishments. This is what makes us stand out from others being considered for the same job. Be specific.

Here are some examples:

> "Reduced turnover in my department by 18 percent."
> "Set up system that doubled the speed of responding to customer queries."
> "Took over a sales region that had lost money three years in a row, and converted it to top sales region in the company in one year."

> "Renegotiated company's health care insurance, saving $130,000 annually in premiums."

Use Key Words

Write the résumé to conform with the requirements of the job you seek. If you are applying for a specific job that has been advertised, study the ad carefully. If it is a job to which you have been referred, obtain as much information about the job from the agency or the person who made the referral. Tailor the résumé to those specifications.

For example, if a job calls for a specific skill such as "designing computer graphics," make sure that phrase is prominently placed in the résumé, even if our experience in this area is minimal.

As employers often receive dozens or even hundreds of résumés, the reader is likely to skim through each one looking for those key words. If the résumé is sent by e-mail or another electronic medium, the employer may just click the key words in the "find" menu and if your résumé doesn't show it, you will not be considered.

Tailor the resume for the specific job. One of the biggest mistakes is sending out a generic resume.

James P. Nolan,
Human Resources Manager

The Ten Don'ts of Résumé Writing

1. *Don't make the résumé too long.* – A résumé should not be an autobiography. Emphasize the major areas of your

background that will help you obtain the interview. Remember, the prospective employer has a limited amount of time. The employer will probably read only those résumés that are clear and concise. Most résumés need not be longer than one page; two pages are permissible for people with extensive work experience. Three is the absolute limit if you really have significant accomplishments.

2. *Don't make the résumé too vague.*– Names, dates and titles are not enough. Offer enough information about your background to give the reader a good idea of why you are worth serious consideration for the position. Don't assume that if the employer wants more information, that he, or she, will call you for it. If others seeking the same position have provided more complete information, you will probably be bypassed. Be sure to include your significant accomplishments.

3. *Don't be negative.*– Granted, everyone's background consists of both positive and negative aspects. However, avoid the negative, or what can be perceived as negative. The following types of information should usually *be omitted* from a résumé:

    a. Personal data such as age, sex, and marital status. (Civil rights laws prohibit asking for this information.)

    b. Height and weight.– People will make judgments about you based on your size. Being small or tall, stout or slim should have no bearing on your ability. Sure, they will see that when you are interviewed. But then their feelings about your appearance will be seen within the context of your overall personality and your experience, and not what they perceive through the eyes of "vital statistics."

c. Reasons for leaving positions.– Although an employer is entitled to know why you left a position, it is better to discuss this at the interview. Except in clear-cut cases, such as "company went out of business," there is usually much more to the story than just a few words can convey. In fact, too little information may result in a negative interpretation. Also, keep in mind that if you state that you wish to change jobs for advancements purposes, it may be interpreted to mean that you were not good enough to advance in your current position.

d. Salary information.– As your salary demands may vary with the job, location, or other factors, it is best to omit your expectations from a résumé.

e. Don't use a photograph.– No matter how good a photo is, it enables the prospective employer to get an impression of us without seeing us. Many people have been denied interviews because of preconceptions. For example, a very good-looking applicant was not invited for an interview because the employer felt he had a "baby face."

4. *Don't list references.*– Most interviewers will ask for references if they are interested in you. Listing them on the résumé takes space that can be used for more significant aspects of your background. You should prepare a list of references to provide if requested. An exception to this is when your reference(s) are persons well known and respected in your field. In this case, including them on

your résumé may enhance your credentials. Always obtain the permission of the person providing the reference before listing him or her on your résumé. .

5. *Don't identify a specific job title desired.*– If you are hoping for a job as a chief chemical engineer, but would consider *other* interesting spots for which you may equally qualify, to head the résumé "chief chemical engineer" would automatically eliminate you from those other opportunities.

6. *Don't start the résumé with "Objective."*– Advertising people have taught us that the emphasis should be placed on the 'you," and not the "I." To sell ourselves to an employer, you must stress what you can do for the employer, not what you want. Instead of saying "My objective is to find a challenging and interesting job." Say, "Offering ten years of progressively more responsible experience in software design." Too much emphasis on "me" is often considered reflective of an immature worker who has a poor work ethic and equally poor attitude.

7. *Don't just update our old résumé.*– When you seek a new position, reevaluate your entire background and rewrite the résumé accordingly.

8. *Don't overplay or underplay education.*– Your educational background information should emphasize that aspect of your schooling that is most pertinent to the position you are seeking. Persons out of school for a relatively short period of time should give more space to education than those out of school for many years. If you are out of school five years or more, succinctly list only college, degree,

and professional credentials. If you have taken courses or seminars related to our field since leaving school, it is a good idea to list the most significant of them.

9. *Don't ruin a well-prepared résumé by utilizing an inappropriate format, or with incorrect spelling, grammatical errors, or sloppy reproduction.–* Proofread, proofread, and proofread. Also, have other people read it, too.

10. *Periodically, review the résumé thoroughly.–* If it appears that the résumé is not generating ample interviews, rewrite it.

Pay very close attention to the specific qualifications an employer lists for a particular job, and make sure your resume or letter contains those exact words.

Gerry Crispin,
Recruiter and Author

Letters of Application

There are two basic approaches while choose composing your letter. One should to send the résumé with a brief transmittal letter. This is considered the more conventional approach; the majority of employers will expect both items. Another approach is to write a more detailed letter, which would be sent instead of the résumé. Although this application style is not as highly favored, it's worth discussing as an alternative in some circumstances. Either type of letter may be sent as a hard copy or as an email.

Cover Letters

A letter of transmittal, or cover letter, can be sent with a résumé in the following situations: William Marshall is the purchasing manager for the Skinner Steel Fabricators in Willets, Ohio. Charles Graham, a member of his network, suggested he send his résumé to Susan Randall, the executive vice president of Standard Tools, Inc. After learning as much as he could about the job and company from Mr Graham and studying the company's website, here is the letter of transmittal that accompanied William's résumé:

Dear Ms Randall,

Charles Graham suggested that I contact you regarding a position in your Purchasing Department.

As you know, Skinner Steel Fabricators, my current employer, is merging with Midwest Metals, and all purchasing will be centralized at Midwest. My experience, as shown in the attached résumé, describes my accomplishment in buying steel and other raw materials similar to those used by Standard Tools. This background will make me a valuable asset to your purchasing staff.

May I have the opportunity of discussing this with you? I will follow up with you next week to see if we might arrange a meeting.

Yours truly,
William Marshall

Enc.: résumé

Note that Marshall immediately stated who referred him. He then pointed out why the recipient's company might have interest in him and asked, point blank, for an interview.

He did *not* review his entire work history in the letter—the enclosed résumé accomplished that. In sending such a letter, be brief and to the point. There is no need to repeat your entire résumé in such correspondence. But, make sure to highlight *some special characteristic* that may be of interest to that firm ("my accomplishment in buying steel and other raw materials similar to those used by Standard Tools"). Close the letter by asking for an interview and follow up with a phone call. This can be time consuming, but if you can get to talk to the person, it greatly increases your chance for success.

Detailed Letters

Some people prefer to write a personal letter describing their qualifications instead of using a résumé. Such letters may be sent to a person to whom you have been referred to, or if you do not have a referral, to an executive in a company that may have a need for someone with your experience.

To whom should these letters be addressed? For an executive position, write to the president or CEO of the company; for a sales position to the sales or marketing manager; for an accounting position to the chief financial officer, and so on.

You can generate personalized letters on your computer for each company on the list. Here is an example of such a letter. Note the reference in the letter to the company by name.

Charles Hawkins
42 Brewster Lane
Greenville, NY 12020

Mr Andrew Carterm,
Blizzard Manufacturing Company,
34 Jay Street,
Schenectady, NY,
12310

Dear Mr Carter,

Is there a place in Blizzard's management for a well-rounded business executive with significant experience in all phases of marketing, manufacturing, employee relations, and finance?

Having risen through the sales ranks to you Vice President of sales for a large manufacturer of hard goods, I was promoted to Vice President in charge of operations and elected to the Board of Directors. In this position I reorganized the entire division along modern management lines, resulting in a significant increase in production with a decrease in administrative costs.

My record of accomplishments includes:

- Conversion of manual production controls to a computer-based program.
- Establishment of workable inventory controls.
- Negotiation of labor contracts that gave the company significant advantages over the former contract.
- Direction of national field sales activities.
- Employment and training of sales, supervisory, and technical personnel.

- Development of a market analysis and forecasting program.
- Coordination of marketing, advertising, and merchandising of products through wholesale, retail, and OEM channels.

With over twenty years of successful achievements, I should make a valuable addition to Blizzard's management team. May I supply you with additional details or arrange an interview at your convenience?

Sincerely,
Charles Hawkins

Some job seekers send out hundreds of these types of letters to lists of companies in their area or their industry. It's usually not profitable to mail letters to an untargeted list of companies, (e.g., the Fortune 500). In general, the giant companies get so many unsolicited letters that they, for the most part, ignore them. On the other hand, mailing letters such as Mr Hawkins' to a list of companies in a specific, targeted industry is likely to obtain some respectable responses. However, as a rule, do not expect tremendous results from any type of unsolicited mail campaign. If we get two or three interviews per hundred letters senty, we are considered to be doing well. So, don't be discouraged by a low response rate. But, don't overlook this avenue, either!

Generally, it is not worth your time to send follow-up letters to the companies you have contacted on your direct-mail list. If the first letter did not elicit a desirable response, a second will usually not succeed any better. However, you may go ahead and make another pass at those few companies on your list in which you have a particular interest.

In this case, telephone the person to whom you sent the original letter (about a week or ten days after he or she should have received it). Ask that person, without seeming too desperate or too pushy, for an interview. Again, the chances are probably slim that they will want to interview you if you have not heard from them already.

Your résumé and/or letter can only open the door for you. In writing either of them, keep in mind that they are your personal sales promotion pieces, and that they should motivate the prospective employer to invite you for an interview.

The Interview

The employment interview is the major phase of the selection process. It is at this point that you are given your only true opportunity to present your case to the prospective employer. If you do not make a favorable impression at the first interview, you are not likely to get another chance.

Most hiring decisions are made after several interviews. A member of the human resources department staff may conduct the first interview for screening purposes. However, subsequent interviews are usually conducted by the individual(s) for whom the candidate will be working. You may see one or more people before you finally meet the decision maker. The decision maker is, usually, the person to whom you will report, or the manager of the department in which you will work. Keep in mind that along the way every interview is important, because if you do not make a favorable impression on each one, the process will be halted, and we may not get to meet the decision maker. Many applicants have lost out because they were holding their best points until meeting with the decision maker, and failed to sell themselves to each interviewer along the way. By underestimating the importance of these preliminary interviews, they forfeited their chance to meet the boss.

Our chances of obtaining the job we are seeking are substantially improved by carefully preparing for each interview.

Arthur R. Pell,
Human Resources Consultant and Author

You must prepare for each interview with utmost care. The first interview is just as important as the last, and vice versa. Assuming that you will be hired because everybody up to the final interview gave the impression that you were a shoo-in—can be a fatal error. Some interviewers may imply that the meeting with the boss is just a routine introduction for the purpose of having him or her "rubber stamp" your employment. Don't fall for this. A negative impression by the higher level manager will inevitably cause a veto of the lower level manager's choice.

Before each interview, rethink your strategy. You can learn much from the earlier interviews—about the types of questions that are likely to be asked and what is most important to the company. Careful analysis of the earlier interviews can aid in preparation for the following interview.

To simplify our overall interviewing discussion, you will use the initial interview as your example. You should prepare for subsequent interviews in the same way that you prepared for the first; adding, of course, the knowledge acquired along the way about the company, the position, and the interviewing techniques favored by previous interviewers.

No interview should ever be taken without first learning as much as you can about what is wanted and expected. Within that light it is equally important to review your own background, given what you can offer so you are ready to present your strengths in a positive, relevant, and convincing manner during your interviews.

The Employer's Objectives

In most instances the interviewer has either read your résumé, or the application form, or both, and already knows the basic outline of your prior work experience and education. In this case, the employment interview will be used to amplify the brief data that most résumés and employment applications provide. During the interview, additional information regarding your duties and responsibilities will be sought. On occasion, the interviewer will not have taken the time to review your background carefully, and it's good to be prepared with a brief overview of your education and experience (of course, particularly as they relate to the position being applied for).

In addition to attempting to learn as much as possible about your work background, the interviewer will be as interested in evaluating your personal characteristics. Among the areas that will be evaluated are your attitude toward your work, your past employers, your direct superiors, and your subordinates. The interviewer will attempt to determine your inner motivations, your short- and long-term goals, and what you have done to date to reach those aspirations. He or she will also be concerned with how you handle special problems at work and what results you have had in resolving difficult situations.

Each position requires special qualifications that may be explored at the interview. You may be asked questions to assess your creativity, your resourcefulness, your ability to sell ideas, how *you get along with others,* your strengths and your weaknesses, and your potential for career growth. Not only will the interviewer listen to what you say, but also he or she will evaluate you on how you say it, what you do not say, and all the nonverbal language clues that you project. In short, the interviewer will want to learn as much as possible about your background, personal characteristics, and inner self during the very short duration of the interview.

Your Objectives

Not only must we be alert to the employer's objectives when going to an employment interview, but we must, also, have our own set of objectives—what we want from the interview—settled in our mind before embarking on each of these interviewing experiences. Your primary objective is to get hired. To facilitate this, your first subordinate objective must be to make a good personal impression on the interviewer. Remember the old adage that first impressions are the most important. Also, be aware that from the first moment you enter the room, everything about you is being assessed and recorded in the mind of the interviewer. His or her impressions can include everything from your clothes, your smile, and your demeanor, to what you say. In other words, "everything you do or say can be used for or against you!"

Your next, subordinate objective is to bring out your strengths in each of the phases of your experience that is discussed. Always minimize your weaknesses. To do this effectively, you must be as knowledgeable, and realistic, of your limitations as you are of your assets. If any of these limitations are brought up, be prepared to indicate how you plan to improve in those areas.

The most important of your subordinate objectives is to remain aware that there are probably several other competitors for the position. Even though you do not know who they are and what they offer, you must be able to present your background so well that you will come across as stronger and better suited for the job than any of the competition.

There are two other related objectives you should keep in mind when being interviewed. One, be sure that this is the right company and the right position for you. (Even the wrong position in the right company or the right position in the wrong company can have devastating consequences.) The other key objective is to set the stage for negotiating the best possible employment deal, should you be made an offer.

With all these goals clearly in mind, and with your knowledge of the company's objectives, you are now ready to plan your interviewing strategy. Again, never go to an employment interview without careful preparation. As discussed earlier in this chapter, obtain as much information about the company as possible. Then, be sure to review your own background. Many successful interviewees report that they made a list of the major aspects of their work history with special emphasis on their accomplishments and that they reread this list before every interview.

Practice is your best bet. If at all possible, rehearse for your employment interviews by engaging in role playing with a friend or career counselor. The more realistic the practice interviews, the more likely you will learn how to handle the more subtle tactics used by real-life interviewers in real-life interviews. Another way to prepare for interviews for the positions you really want is to accept interviews by anyone who wants to interview you, even if you are not particularly interested in the opportunity. These real-life encounters will work to sharpen your interviewing skills, build your self-confidence, and, generally, make you more effective when faced with the interviews that are really important to you.

Planning and Preparing for the Interview

1. Do your homework. Research the industry, organization, and the individual(s) with whom you are interviewing.

2. Know the organization's place in the industry.

3. Prepare a succinct answer for common, difficult, and challenging interview questions. Examples of some of these are given later in this chapter.

4. Be prepared for both a one-on-one interview, and also a group interview.

5. Prepare specific examples and evidence of the knowledge, skills, and positive attitude we possess.

6. Prepare questions for the interviewer(s) that demonstrates your knowledge and eagerness to work for them.

7. Practice with someone you trust to provide honest feedback.

When you are asked if you can do a job, tell 'em, "Certainly I can!" Then get busy and find out how to do it.

Theodore Roosevelt

Common Interview Questions

The following are examples of interview questions that are frequently asked. Notice that they are all open ended; they cannot be answered with a one-word response.

1. How would you describe yourself?
2. Why did you leave your last job?
3. What made you choose this line of work?
4. What are your long-range and short-range goals?
5. What kind of recognition and rewards are important to you?
6. What specific goals, other than those related to your occupation, have you established?
7. What do you see yourself doing five years from now?
8. What do you expect to be earning in five years?
9. Can you explain this gap in your employment history?
10. What are your thoughts about working alone versus working with teams?
11. How do you work under pressure?
12. How would you evaluate your ability to deal with conflict?
13. Have you ever had difficulty with a supervisor? How did you resolve this problem?

14. What do you consider to be your greatest strengths and weaknesses?

15. How would a good friend describe you?

16. Describe the best job you've ever had.

17. Describe the best supervisor you've ever had.

18. What would your last boss say about your work performance?

19. Why should I hire you?

20. What do you think it takes to be successful in an organization like ours?

21. In what ways do you think you can make a contribution to our organization?

22. What do you enjoy doing in your spare time?

23. What qualities should a successful manager possess?

24. Describe the relationship that should exist between the supervisor and those reporting to him or her?

25. What accomplishments have given you the most satisfaction? Why?

26. What can you tell us about our organization?

27. What interests you about our service or products?

28. What can you tell me about our competitors?

In a job interview, you may be up against nine competitors. Be ready to state your focus more clearly than your nine rivals. Know your focus or get beaten by the competition who knows theirs.

Alan Fox,
Sociologist

Anticipate Difficult Questions

On occasion you may be asked a particularly challenging question, such as for an explanation about a job that you held for a short period, or for a creative solution to a hypothetical problem. If you are, you should simply do your best to answer the question answer without getting upset in any way. The following tips apply to when you are asked a difficult question:

> Show a genuine interest and desire to understand the question by listening carefully and, if needed, asking for clarification.

> Welcome the challenge. Thank him or her for the question and compliment the question.

> Don't take the question personally or get defensive. Remember, every question indicates interest.

> Stay calm, keep your emotions in check, and breathe.

> Smile, maintain eye contact, and use confident gestures.

> Lighten things up by using appropriate levity.

> Pick up on and respond to key words by weaving them into our answer.

> Relate an incident or story that has a positive outcome.

> Wherever possible, include a specific example of an accomplishment related to the subject under discussion.

Interview Dos and Don'ts

Human resource professionals have reported on some of the things applicants do that turn them on or off when it comes to that person.

Dos

1. Arriving on time or appropriately early.
2. Turning off cell phone and other electronic devices.
3. Dressing professionally.
4. Establishing rapport with the interviewer by taking a sincere interest in something in his or her office.
5. Maintaining eye contact and using appropriate body language when speaking to the interviewer.
6. Being a good listener and watching for nonverbal cues.
7. Showing enthusiasm and positive energy.
8. Speaking kindly of others.
9. Saying "we" and assuming that we have the job.
10. Being clear and concise when answering questions.
11. Providing specific evidence and examples to back up our claims.
12. Providing only solid and current references who can verify our qualifications.
13. Asking pertinent and thoughtful questions, such as:
    - Is there anything I can do between now and starting the job to help with the transition?
    - Are there any challenges of the job that I can prepare for in advance?
    - Are there materials I can review or suggested reading to familiarize myself with the organization, the people, or the culture?
    - Do you have any reservations or concerns about me or my qualifications that I can address now?
    - What is the next step?
    - When I can expect a decision?

Don'ts

1. Arriving late.
2. Leaving cell phones or any other device on while in the interview, even in silent mode.
3. Appearing messy or poorly groomed.
4. Being too assertive, aggressive, or intrusive.
5. Seeming preoccupied, too relaxed, or uncomfortable making eye contact.
6. Thinking about what you want to say while the interviewer is talking instead of concentrating on what the interviewer is asking or saying.
7. Demonstrating a lack of energy.
8. Talking negatively about former employers, colleagues, or experiences.
9. Talking down about yourself or showing a lack of self-confidence.
10. Appearing more interested in salary, benefits, or holidays than the job.
11. Being vague or making empty statements about your qualifications, rambling on, or seeming unsure about what you are saying.
12. Worrying about appearing nervous. A little nervousness is natural and shows that you care and want to make a good impression.
13. Giving outdated or irrelevant names for references.
14. Leaving topics unresolved.

Following Up on the Interview

When we leave the interview, we want to make sure that we are remembered and have made a good impression. To do this:

1. Write a thank-you note to all those who interviewed you. Err on the side of thoroughness. Two to three sentences, in which you tell the person you enjoyed meeting them and hope to work with them, is appropriate.
2. Whether handwritten or through email, make each thank-you note a little different.
3. If someone on the administrative staff was particularly helpful, consider mentioning this in the thank-you note.
4. If you do not hear anything in the timeframe that was promised, a phone call is appropriate to check the status of the position.
5. When leaving a phone message, be brief and state your name and phone number at the beginning and end of the message.
6. If the interviewers are still in the decision-making stage, consider offering something unusual or unique, such as going out for a day in the field with one of their employees, spending a day at the office, or providing them with an action plan on a matter discussed at the interview.
7. Let your references know that you offered their names and tell them about the position for which you applied.

Be Open to Feedback

Perhaps the most challenging aspect of managing your external image is the difficulty in seeing yourself as others see you.

Research indicates that we are probably more critical of ourselves than others are of us. At the same time, we may be unaware of negative behaviors that need to be corrected.

Some ways to gain an accurate view of your own external image include:

> Seeing and listening to yourself on video recordings.
> Looking objectively in the mirror. Are you well shaven, and neat in your appearance? Are your clothes wrinkled or ill fitting?
> Asking trusted colleagues for honest input.
> Monitoring others' reactions.

Friends, particularly fellow job seekers, provide an invaluable opportunity to solicit feedback. And, we represent the same resource for each of them.

Cast ourselves in the role of coach and mentor. Become more conscious of the impressions you are forming about others and try to isolate the cues that create those impressions. Then, practice sharing your observations in a diplomatic, tactful, and constructive way.

Sum and Substance

> Before writing the résumé, you should carefully review your entire background with emphasis on your accomplishments thus far in your career.
> The ten don'ts of résumé writing:
>   1. Don't make the résumé too long.
>   2. Don't make the résumé too vague.
>   3. Don't be negative.

4. Don't list references.

5. Don't identify a specific job title desired.

6. Don't start the résumé with "Objective."

7. Don't just update our old résumé.

8. Don't overplay or underplay education.

9. Don't ruin a well-prepared résumé by using an inappropriate format, or with incorrect spelling, grammatical errors, or sloppy reproduction.

10. Thoroughly review the résumé.

➤ Keep in mind that your résumé and/or letter are your personal sales promotion pieces, and that they should motivate the prospective employer to invite you for an interview.

➤ The employment interview is the major phase of the selection process. It is at this point that you are given the only true opportunity to present your case to a prospective employer. If you do not make a favorable impression at the *first interview*, you are not likely to get another chance.

➤ Never give an interview without first learning as much as you can about what is wanted and expected by the employer. Review your own background for what you have to offer so that you are ready to present your strengths in a positive, relevant, and convincing manner.

➤ If at all possible, rehearse for your employment interviews by engaging in role-playing with a friend or career counselor. Get feedback on your interviewing skills from tapes or videos of your rehearsals and comments from colleagues.

➤ You must prepare for each interview with utmost care. The first interview is just as important as the last, and vice versa.

➤ Before each interview, rethink your strategy. You can

learn much from the earlier interviews—about the types of questions that are likely to be asked and what is most important to the company.

> Before each interview, review the commonly asked questions and dos and don'ts of interviewing presented in this chapter.

> Send a follow-up letter after each interview, stating thanks for the interview and a brief comment to emphasize one or two of your strong points.

10

CHANGE CAREERS IN
MIDSTREAM

What is it that you like doing? If you don't like it, get
out of it, because you'll be lousy at it. You don't have
to stay with a job for the rest of your life, because if
you don't like it you'll never be successful in it.

Lee Iacocca,
Former chairman, Chrysler Corporation

If you cannot reach your career goals in your current profession, you may find it advisable to make a complete change in your career. History abounds with people whose fame was gained in their second careers. Gauguin was a bank clerk before finding his career as a painter. Benjamin Franklin started his work-life as a printer. Dale Carnegie was a salesman and actor before becoming a teacher and author.

Most cases of career change, of course, are not as dramatic as with famous persons. An engineer becomes a photographer; a teacher returns to school and studies medicine; a salesman shifts to advertising copywriting or a retailer starts a new career as a clergyman.

There are many reasons people desire to change occupations or professions after spending many years of education and experience developing their skills in their original fields.

1. Dead ends: Because of either poor planning or a bad break, a person may reach a point in his or her professional development from which there is no opportunity to go any further. A salesperson may be the best on the staff, but cannot move into management; a nurse may find she has neither the background nor inclination to pass beyond a certain level. If you cannot advance in your profession and are not content to settle at the level you can reach, you may wish to seriously consider a complete change.

2. Change of conditions leading to professional advancement: When we chose to enter our field, we may have based our career plan on conditions that exist in our industry. Because of changing conditions, you may no longer be satisfied with this choice. Industries become obsolete or downgraded in importance because of technological advances or other reasons. Professional specialties important in one decade are less important ten years later.

3. Industrial recessions: Sometimes there are temporary or even long run periods of recession in a particular industry. When the cold war ended with the demise of the Soviet Union, the US government deemphasized the aerospace program and simultaneously cut back on defense spending. The professions that depended on these industries were badly hit by recession. Engineers, physicists, and other scientists, as well as administrative personnel in these areas could not find jobs at all related to their experience. Career change was a necessity for many of them. More recently, the downturn in the residential and commercial real estate markets has resulted in the unemployment or underemployment of many people— carpenters, architects, real estate agents, and decorators have all felt the impact in their work lives. A good number of these people have been forced to create new careers for themselves.

4. Personal reasons: People frequently change careers because of unhappiness or boredom in their current fields. Some psychologists have recommended that to have a more exciting and rewarding life, you should change careers two or three times in your lives. However, this is not practical for most people. There is no justification for changing careers because of temporary displeasure with your work. As stated earlier in this book, decisions as important as a job or career change should not be made lightly. It is not unusual for a person to become bored with a job he or she does day after day, year after year. Most jobs entail some degree of monotony. The challenge of a new career excites some people. But this alone is not an adequate reason to change careers. The answer may better lie in

seeking more challenge in your current company or by making a job change in your own field. (Often the greener grass in someone else's profession only looks green from afar.) Every field has its boring aspects, and we might be just as unhappy if you shift.

To love what you do and feel that it matters—how could anything be more fun?

Katharine Graham,
Publisher

Choosing Your Next Career

Changing careers is never an easy task. The older you get, the more years you have in your present profession, and, in all likelihood, the higher your salary. This factor alone may make shifting into another field somewhat unappealing. However, once you have made the decision, you have to be prepared for hard work, perhaps years of reeducation and study, sacrifice in terms of money, time, and effort, and many disappointments along the way to achieving your new goal. Professional help is available for people desiring career advice. Most people think of career guidance as limited to students in their early career planning. Actually, career counseling can be of value to persons at any age seeking this type of assistance.

Career counselors assist clients in several ways. Most use various types of aptitude, personality, and interest tests to identify areas of potential that may not have been obvious to the individual, e.g., an engineer who concentrated on preparing for and working in a special discipline may not have consciously recognized possession of capabilities for communications or creativity, or other assets that are valuable in completely different areas. Unlike the tests one takes when applying for a job, the purpose of these tests is not to disqualify us, but to aid you in understanding your potential.

In addition to testing, most counselors will delve into your thinking and attitudes about various types of work, as well as your interests and activities not related to your career. They will want to know about your hobbies, civic, and social activities, extra-curricular interests when you were in school, the occupational backgrounds and interests of your spouse, and those of members of your family and friends.

All of these give them insight into facets of your personality that can help them identify new careers or new ways of orienting your current career that will utilize these findings.

Career counselors will rarely point out one specific type of work and suggest that you make this your career goal. They will usually provide a broad picture of the areas in which you most likely will be happy and successful. They will then give you some specific information about the requirements to enter these fields and where you can obtain direct information about them.

Burt, at age 30 has been a moderately successful insurance salesman for eight years. He is stymied in his growth and feels that he just cannot face another twenty-five years doing this work.

His tests show a strong artistic talent. His hobbies have been in creative areas (stage design for the local theater, and arts and crafts counselor for the Cub Scouts).

The career counselor recommended several areas that would

utilize Burt's talents. They included interior design, fashion coordination, merchandising, teaching of art and some others.

Burt decided to investigate interior design and fashion coordination. The counselor guided him to persons and organizations in these fields to enable him to learn more about the work and the additional education and background he would have to acquire to qualify for these careers.

> *The people who get on in this world are the people who get up and look for the circumstances they want, and, if they can't find them, make them.*
>
> *George Bernard Shaw*

Professional career guidance should be obtained from specially trained persons in this field. To locate a qualified career guidance specialist, check first with local colleges and universities. They often have career guidance services at the school or can suggest reputable counselors. Agencies or professional associations provide such services in nearly all countries around the world.

Making the Change

There are several approaches to career change that may be applicable. In addition to the two we'll discuss immediately, you can also start your own business, which will be addressed later in this chapter.

Choosing a Related Occupation

Making a move into a field similar to the one that you're in is the easiest route to follow. It utilizes your past education and experience to the greatest extent and redirects it to a different phase of work. An example is Carl, who changed careers by moving from a design engineer to a sales engineer. Such a change used all of his engineering education and experience, yet he is really in a completely new field. Selling a technical product gives him the opportunity to use his strengths in engineering and his interests and aptitudes in dealing with people.

Your first step is to analyze our background, either by introspection or with the help of a human resources professional or a career specialist. Study fields that may be of interest to you. Once you have selected one or more occupational areas, identify those aspects of your background that are related or transferable to the new field. This prepares you to use them in selling ourselves to a company in the new field. Although the employer is likely to tend to stress on the differences in your background from the job specifications, you have the tools available to show how the similarities outweigh the differences. Don't overlook the intangibles that play an important a role in job success: drive, stability, intelligence, perseverance, and the like.

Choose a job you love, and you will never have to work a day in your life.

Confucius

Complete Career Change

A complete change of career is much more difficult than a move into a related field. It may require extensive retraining or education. If you now are a chemist and want to become a lawyer, you have to go to law school for at least three years.

Even changing from one discipline in the chemical field to another may take months or years of added study. Other professional areas have similar educational requirements.

In some instances new occupations can be learned on the job. But this usually involves taking a lower level job than you have and much less money. It may also mean many months of retraining, even though you are employed.

You must weigh the advantages of a career change against the difficulties in accomplishing the change when making your choice.

Professional career advice as discussed above is strongly recommended.

Your work is to discover your work and then with all your heart to give yourself to it.

Buddha

Whether or not you use professional counseling, there is much you can do on your own to assure that you have adequate information before making the final decision.

> *Research:* There is material available about every type of career. Read several books about the work, the people in it, and the like. Check the subject index in your library, write to the trade or professional associations, and pick up the trade magazines or professional journals.
> *Websites:* Read the websites of several of the companies in the field. This will provide much information about their products or services, types of positions, markets, and other valuable facts about the industry. Search online for articles

and blogs written by those who are involved in the kind of work that interests you.

› *Networking:* Even more important than reading is to visit with persons in the field of interest. Start with friends or relatives. Even if they are not in your field of interest, they may be able to introduce you to persons they know in the field. In addition, contact local companies where such people are employed. Make every effort to meet with individuals working in the profession of interest. Most persons are willing to give you a few minutes of their time for this purpose. If you cannot find anyone who can help you, phone, or write to the editor of the trade or professional magazine in the field requesting an interview, or for referrals to members of the profession.

You can learn much from an interview with persons in the field that may not be given in books. They can tell you about the day-to-day problems, and the frustrations as well as the satisfactions of the working conditions, promotional opportunities, and financial rewards of the profession. You can also discover how easy or difficult it is to obtain entry-level jobs, to make job changes, and the like.

If possible, ask for an opportunity to observe a typical day's work. See what it is like to perform this type of work. You may discover that many of the points that attracted you to this career are minor and are outweighed by factors that do not attract you. It is better to learn the downside of a profession before embarking on a new career. On the other hand, a detailed investigation such as this may reinforce your interest and be the key determinant in your choice of a new career.

Your success in your career will be in direct proportion to what you do after you've done what you are expected to do.

Brian Tracey,
Author and Motivational Consultant

Examples of Career Change Successes

The following stories describe the paths some people have taken to move from one type of career to the next.

Mike—From Engineer to Physician

Mike was a mechanical engineer working as a design engineer with a leading aircraft manufacturer. He felt stymied in growth and unhappy in his work. After much introspection and study he decided to look into medicine and dentistry—even though it would take years of added study. Mike read all he could about each field and spoke at length to dentists and physicians. He visited medical and dental schools to determine if he would qualify for admission and whether they felt a man with his background and at his age could make such a major transition. He took the MCAT and DAT (the admissions tests for medical and dental school) and scored very high on them.

The key factor that worked was a long discussion with the director of a major hospital. He was able to clarify many of his doubts and learn the hard facts of a life devoted to such a career.

Mike chose medicine. At age thirty, he recognized he had to make a major time and financial sacrifice. He arranged the necessary financing for tuition and support of his wife and children. He was admitted without difficulty to a fine medical college because his engineering education and background were considered excellent preparation for medical study. He completed his medical education, internship and residency with honors. He reported that medical school was no more difficult than engineering school had been—and with his added maturity, perhaps less so. Today Mike is a highly successful (and happy) anesthesiologist. His engineering experience has enabled him to contribute many ideas and innovations to medical practice.

In making a major career change, such as Mike did, you must not only look into the potential in the field and your interests and aptitude for it, but also consider the additional preparation it may take and how you can finance it. Most fields require added education that costs money for the tuition itself, plus the loss or reduction of income during training. This must be carefully planned and discussed with your family. They, too, must make the sacrifice. Only after this can you make this important decision.

> *Think not of yourself as the architect of your career but as the sculptor. Expect to have to do a lot of hard hammering and chiseling and scraping and polishing.*
>
> *B.C. Forbes,*
> *Publisher*

Kimberly—From Market Researcher to Math Teacher

Kimberly was a market research analyst in a pharmaceutical company for five years. She was a competent statistician and had reached the top of the salary scale for that position. In order to advance in marketing, she would have to obtain experience in sales. Kimberly had no interest in sales, but had always been intrigued by the idea of teaching. She knew there was a demand for math teachers, so she explored this field. After obtaining much information about the teaching field and its requirements, she made her analysis. She used a simple system. She divided a paper into two columns. In one she listed the requirements, and in the other, her background. Then she compared the columns to determine what she lacked in order to qualify.

Kimberly's chart:

My Background	Job Requirements
Education:	
B.A. Major Math	B.A. – Math
MBA Marketing	Courses in Education
	State Certificate in Teaching.
Experience	I year Student teaching
Statistical analysis	Helpful: Work using advanced math
Writing reports	
Training new employees	

Kim realized that she had to go back to school for the courses in education. She enrolled in a night and weekend program leading to an MA in education at a local college. With transfer credits from her MBA courses in statistics and work experience in her market research job, she completed the master's program in eighteen months. She resigned her job to take a student-teaching assignment. She passed the certification exam and was hired immediately as a high school math teacher.

Jim—From Fighter Pilot to Minister

Jim flew fighter planes in both wars in Iraq. He was decorated for bravery and moved up the ranks in the Air Force to Lt Colonel. He chose to retire after twenty years of service. Jim had enjoyed the Air Force and still loved flying, and although he could have accepted several offers from airlines, he chose to make a radical career change.

As a child, Jim attended church regularly, but after college, he rarely went to services. During the second Iraq war, Jim was forced to make a crash landing. His copilot and gunman were killed, but Jim survived with only minor injuries. Jim credited his survival to God and planned to devote his life to serving Him. When he returned home, he was assigned to an Air Force facility in the New York area. He took an active role in a local church and spent much of his free time working there. At his pastor's suggestion, Jim began studying for the ministry. He took night courses at a college in the area. When he retired, he went full-time to the Union Theological Seminary. After his ordination, he was called to a church in Pennsylvania, where he is fully engaged in the work he loves.

Andrew—From Policeman to Mortician

Andrew made two career shifts. After high school he became an apprentice toolmaker, but realized early that factory work was not for him. He felt he wanted a job in which he would work with people, not things. Police work seemed interesting, so he enrolled in the police science program at a community college. After getting his associate's degree, he passed the police exam and was hired as a police officer in his hometown.

Andrew enjoyed police work, and although he was promoted to detective, he felt that this was not how he wanted to spend his life. One of his friends worked in a local funeral home, and Andrew often visited his facility and became interested in that field. He saw how the funeral director and his staff helped people who were experiencing some of the worst moments of their lives to make decisions and cope with their sorrow. He decided that he would like to do that. He went back to the community college and obtained another associate's degree, this is time in mortuary science.

Andrew chose to remain in the police department, and worked a second job at a mortuary. It worked out well and a few years later, while still on the police force, he opened his own funeral home and managed it as a part-time business. After twenty-one years in the police force, he finally retired and is now a full-time funeral director. His enthusiasm for his work has made him one of the most respected funeral directors in his town. In addition, his son chose to follow his father and now owns two funeral homes in a neighboring town. And last year, his twenty-one-year-old grandson joined him in his business.

Don't Give Up

Persons desiring a complete redirection of their professional life may find it extremely difficult. Sometimes they never can make the change. However, the reason for failure is not always lack of ability or even the prejudice against persons who are not experienced in a field, a strong, deep-seated bias that defeats a good number of career-change seekers. The reason often is that the career changer gives up too soon.

Changing careers takes a lot of hard work and extensive exposure to potential employers. Most of this must be done on our own in as creative a way as possible.

Never continue in a job you don't enjoy. If you're happy in what you're doing, you'll like yourself, you'll have inner peace. And if you have that, along with physical health, you'll have more success than you could possibly have imagined.

Roger Caras,
TV Commentator and Author

A Business Of Your Own

Sometimes the best method of changing careers is to start a business of your own. Perhaps you have a product or an idea that you wish to develop, or perhaps you just desire to be your own boss and operate a factory, store, or service business.

Most doors are open and you can enter the field of your choice—so long as you have the money to do so.

Business means investment. Do not even think of a business of your own unless you have carefully analyzed what it takes in capital, working expenses and reserves. Also consider that in most businesses, you may have to forgo taking a salary for many months until it is underway. Business also involves risk. If we fail, we not only have lost our income for that period, but possibly our savings and that of our backers.

On the other hand, the payoff to running your own business can be substantial. Not only can you make a large amount of money, but you can accrue equity, which builds up your estate. A good business can always be sold at a profit.

There are many intangible rewards as well, such as the satisfaction one gets from making the final decisions and being one's own boss. However, you must accept that the hours are usually long; there is much work to do and problems about which to worry. In choosing which business to enter, be sure that you have the knowledge needed to operate it or can obtain this know-how rapidly. The main cause of business failure other than lack of capital is lack of knowledge.

Should I Go into Business for Myself?

Do I have the aptitude needed to successfully operate my own business? In order to decide on this important matter, answer the following questions honestly. Do not try to fit yourself into a pattern.

Perhaps you may ask a close friend to rate you on the same questionnaire. Be sure to identify your weak spots. If correctable, take steps to do something about them. If not, perhaps you should not go into business for yourself.

Check the statement under each category that best fits us:

Am I a self-starter?

- I do things on my own. Nobody has to tell me to get going.
- If someone gets me started, I keep going.
- Easy does it. I don't push myself until I have to.

What kind of person am I socially?

- I like people. I can get along with just about anybody.
- I have plenty of friends. I don't need anybody else.
- Most people bug me.

Can I lead others?

- I can get most people to go along when I start something.
- I can give the orders if someone else tells me what to do.
- I let someone else get things moving. Then I go along if I feel like it.

Can I take responsibility?

- I like to take charge of things and see them through.
- I'll take over if I have to, but I'd rather let someone else be responsible.
- There's always some eager beaver around wanting to show how smart he is. I say, let him.

How well do I organize a project?

- I like to have a plan before I start. I'm usually the one to get things lined up when the gang wants to do something.
- I do all right unless things get too goofed up. Then I cop out.
- I get all set and then something comes along and blows the whole bag. So I just take things as they come.

How dedicated am I as a worker?

- I can keep going as long as I need to. I don't mind working hard for something I want.
- I'll work hard for a while, but when I've had enough, that's it.
- I can't see that hard work gets you anywhere.

Can I make decisions?

- I can make up my mind in a hurry if I have to. It usually turns out okay too.
- I can if I have plenty of time. If I have to make up my mind fast, I think later I should have decided the other way.
- I don't like to be the one who has to decide things. I'd probably blow it.

Can people trust what I say?

- Certainly. I don't say things I don't mean.
- I try to be on the level most of the time, but sometimes I say what's easiest.
- Why does it matter if the other person doesn't know the difference?

Can I stick with something even when it is hard?

- If I make up my mind to do something, I don't let anything stop me.
- I usually finish what I start—if it doesn't get fouled up. If something doesn't go right from the start, I turn off.
- I never run down!
- I have enough energy for most things I want to do.
- I run out of juice sooner than most of my friends seem to.

How many checks are there beside the first answer to each question? How many checks are there beside the second answer to each question? How many checks are there beside the third answer to each question?

If most of the checks are beside the first answers, you probably have what it takes to run a business. If not, you're likely to have more trouble than you can handle by yourself, and you might be better off if you find a partner who is strong on the points you are weak on. If many checks are beside the third answer, not even a good partner will be able to help you.

> *Starting out to make money is the greatest mistake in life. Do what you feel you have a flair for doing, and if you are good enough at it, the money will come.*
>
> Greer Garson,
> Actor

Selecting the Business to Enter

In selecting the type of business to enter, try to utilize your past experience and interests, rather than going into a completely strange business. If you have always had a hobby of photography, a camera store, commercial photography, or a related field might be a possible business venture for you.

If in your past job you were responsible for recruiting and employing personnel, starting an employment agency would be logical. If you are a good mechanic, you might find an appliance or equipment repair business a good opportunity.

On the other hand, businesses in which you have had no experience or knowledge can still be successful, if you have a sincere interest and aptitude, and facilities are available to teach you the details of the operation.

Most small businesses fall into three categories: manufacturing, marketing, and service.

In manufacturing, we make and sell a product. The required capital investment varies with the type of manufacturing. The type of business usually requires investment in equipment and materials, as well as rental of space and the employment of skilled and semi-skilled personnel. A manufacturing business is usually attractive to persons who have worked in manufacturing companies, such as engineers, production executives, and persons with mechanical orientation.

Marketing may take the form of wholesale or retail operations, and involves selling. The wholesale marketer may have to invest in inventory of merchandise, warehouse space, and the employment of sales and warehousing personnel. Retailers have to invest in store fixtures and displays, an inventory of merchandise, the rental of space in a high traffic area and the employment of sales clerks. A small retail haberdashery can be started in a residential neighborhood with a few thousand dollars, but a midtown clothing store would cost tens of thousands to start up, and a discount or department store might involve a very significant investment.

Service businesses are the least expensive to enter. They take very little capital, as little or no equipment is needed. Examples:

> Sales agency—Running a sales business does not require us to purchase stock or inventory. Once an order is sold, the manufacturer or wholesaler ships from their stock. This type

of opportunity appeals to salespeople or others with sales aptitude.

› Consulting—Often business executives or professionals (engineers, accountants, human resource specialists, and the like) feel they could succeed in a business by consulting in their specialty. The capital investment is low; we need to just rent of an office, purchase furniture, create a website, print some stationery and promotional material, and find ways to advertise our services. We can get into consulting with just enough money to pay our first few month's bills. However, it is not easy to build a clientele. The reason so many consultants fail is not lack of capability, but the inability to obtain new business. Unless we know enough potential clients, consulting is too risky for most persons.

› Business services—Many different types of business services are needed. A business of this nature is a good and relatively inexpensive way to get into business on our own. Based on our own interests and talents, there are countless services to consider: web design and upkeep services, printing and duplicating services, direct-mail promotion, bookkeeping and accounting services for other small businesses, employment agencies, temporary employment services, credit and collection bureaus, etc. If we can uncover a need for a needed service, we may have a business in it.

•   Consumer services—Other types of service businesses serve the consumer. There is an insatiable demand for people who can make repairs, help individuals with special problems such as tax services, home maintenance, fitness trainers, musical instrument sales and repair, teaching of music, art, languages, technical matters, etc.

The area of business you choose should fit your own interests and aptitudes, but it should also be carefully researched to assure that there is a need for it. Visit with prospective consumers or clients. Determine how well the market is covered now. If other similar businesses are doing well, is there room for one more? If your competition is not successful or seems to be covering the market, are you planning to offer a better product or service to assure you will succeed? Get all the facts before making a decision.

Do you have the resources to start your own operation? Check again on how much money it takes to get started and build up to a point where you can start drawing money from the new business. Be sure you can manage this. Unless there is no doubt about your capability to finance the business and your family's needs until the business gets off the ground, do not even attempt to start.

Getting Started

There are three methods of getting started in one's own business: starting from scratch, buying a going business or an interest in one, or obtaining a franchise.

> *You have power over your mind—not outside events. Realize this, and you will find strength.*
>
> Marcus Aurelius,
> Roman Emperor and Philosopher

Starting from Scratch

When you start your own business from the ground up, you

must use your own best judgment, resources, and skills to develop the enterprises. Advantages: One advantage to starting your own business is that costs may be relatively low, as there is no initial sales price or franchise free. As you do not have these capital investments, you have more money for working capital or purchasing initial equipment. You reap the full profit, as there are no royalties or other obligatory fees to be paid.

Limitations: When you start a new business from scratch, it generally takes a longer time to become established. Customers tend to patronize established or well-known firms over new businesses. In order to make a name in your area, you must work much harder and spend more money on advertising and sales promotion than if you buy an established business or a reputed franchise. No matter how good your product or service, you must take time to get the potential customers to know about it. You're likely to make typical trial and error mistakes, but if an experienced person is able to teach you the business, you may avoid making too many errors. As a rule, when starting your own business it will take a while to carve out a share of the market sufficient to support you.

Buying an Established Business

One may overcome some of the problems of starting from the beginning by either purchasing an established business outright or buying an interest in one.

Advantages: A helpful aspect of buying an established business is that it has active customers and produces immediate income for you. If it is a profitable company, much of the groundwork is already completed. You have customers, suppliers, a line of credit, and other matters that take a new business a long time to develop. If you have purchased a part of a business (as a partner), you have access to the training and guidance of the original owner.

Limitations: In buying a business outright, you might be buying a going business, but it may be going down instead of up. This is not necessarily a reason not to purchase the business, but it is a warning that you should investigate carefully. If the reason for its decline is a factor that you can correct (e.g., more careful management, additional capital, etc.) it may be a very good buy. However, if the reason is a poor product, bad reputation, or inferior facilities or location, you may be wise to decline the deal.

Be sure to check the performance record of the company. Does it have a number of clients? What are its costs and profits? What is its reputation in the community? This can be checked through the local chamber of commerce, or Better Business Bureau. It can also be verified by talking to persons who may be users of the business' goods or services.

Consult your accountants to help you evaluate the worth of the proposed sale. They can give you guidelines as to whether the price asked is reasonable and also analyze the company's finances to see how it has been operated and if there are hidden problems from a financial viewpoint. Determine what assets you will get. What sort of training will we receive? Except in unusual circumstances such as serious illness or death, some training should be given as part of the deal. Does the current owner have employees who will remain with company? Of course, one cannot guarantee an employee will stay on after a change in ownership, but you should discuss this thoroughly with the original owner and staff. Be sure you have a clear picture of what equipment, fixtures, inventory, and the like are part of the deal. Be sure they are valued at reasonable figures. Often a business' property is carried on the books at inflated prices. Have your accountants carefully review these figures. If there is a price for the company's goodwill (the excess of the purchase price of a company over its book value, an intangible asset), make sure that you agree about its value. Above all, be sure you have a clear understanding of who is to pay outstanding debts and accounts payable. There are countless details that only your accountants and attorney can fully appreciate. It pays to hire competent professional help in buying a business. This is not the place to save money.

Many businesses require specialized knowledge, and a specialized lawyer or accountant can be far more helpful than a general practitioner. For example, if the business requires a license from the government (e.g., a liquor store, or an employment, real estate, or insurance agency) a lawyer who is familiar with the licensing procedure can considerably expedite the start-up or transaction. If the business is based on a patent or a licensing arrangement with a patent holder, the attorney with a general practice will not be as helpful as a specialist in patent law. The same holds true for accountants where special know-how in an industry may be invaluable.

To locate such specialists, check with their trade or professional association. Another source are persons currently in the field either as competitors or related businesses. They are often willing to suggest a lawyer or accountant to you.

If no special circumstances exist, any legitimate lawyer or accountant should be able to assist you in your business. It is not necessary to hire the services of major law or accounting firms. Local bar and accounting associations can suggest reputable people in their membership. The bank in which you have your account might also be a good source for referrals. Once you choose the attorney and accountant, be as frank with him or her as you would be with your physician. Divulge all of your concepts and plans about the new business if we want the best advice.

Remember, however, you are the decision makers. Do not expect business decisions from these specialists—only advice and counsel in their field of expertise.

If you are buying a portion of a business and the current owner will be your partner, you have the advantage of the smooth continuation of the business and the availability of an experienced colleague to train and consult with you. However, you must be very sure that you can work together and have compatible personalities. A business partnership is like a marriage. Your life can be miserable if you do not get along well.

You must also be assured that the person has a record of success that you can help make stronger. If your new colleague is a weakling, clutching onto you and your additional financial support to save a poor business, joining his business is probably not a good move.

In any partnership arrangement (or purchase of shares in a corporation) make sure your attorney draws up or approves any contract to assure that your investment and control are properly protected.

Franchising

Obtaining a franchise is the third alternative that can be followed in starting a new business. In considering this route to a business of your own, look first for those franchisors that offer the kind of business you wish to operate. There are so many different kinds of businesses offered that you really have a wide choice. Go to franchise exhibitions (they are held all over the country), send for literature, and check the Internet. There are a wide variety of businesses to choose from, one of which might meet your new career goals.

Once you choose the field you want, select the franchisor and determine if it is reputable. Determine what you will receive for the franchise fee, what training they will give, what equipment or inventory, and what type of continual service after the opening.

You should visit as many of the organization's franchisees as possible. Find out whether the operators are satisfied with the services they are getting from the franchisor. Meeting with other owners will also show you the caliber of the people they have been able to attract.

Before making a decision as to which franchise is best for you, have your accountant check the company's financial status and have your attorney examine the contract. Be sure that the franchise fee and any other financial obligations are understood and are competitive with other franchisors. The least expensive arrangement is not necessarily the best one. Be sure what you will get for your money is what you need and expect.

Advantages: Good franchisors help us in every step of the way. They will help in selecting and setting up a suitable facility, establish a realistic budget, train you and your initial staff, offer counsel on all phases of the business, and give you the value of their name as an established business. In brief, they will help you get underway much faster than you could on your own.

Limitations: You will probably need a larger capital investment to run a franchise than if you create your own business. Franchise fees vary considerably with the type of business. Most franchisors will arrange for financing part of the franchise fee. In addition to the fee, you may have to agree to purchase equipment, fixtures, etc., and commit yourself to purchasing materials and supplies from the franchisor. In service businesses, franchisors usually charge a royalty on our total business receipts. Before agreeing to buy a franchise, ascertain just what your obligations are and be sure you understand them.

Another feature of franchising that may be disadvantageous is that some franchisors maintain strict control over their franchisees. You must do a minimum business or lose the franchise. Be sure you are cognizant of this and that the expected profits are reasonable. It is usual for this minimum to be waived for the start-up period, and you may want to insist on this term.

Sum and Substance

Changing careers may be one of the most important steps you take in your life. Whether you shift to a career close to your current profession or move to an entirely new field, whether you do this via a job change or in your own business, be very sure you analyze the move objectively and make your decision based on hard, sound facts.

➤ Decisions as important as a job or career change should not be made lightly. There is no justification for changing careers because of temporary displeasure with our work.

➤ Changing careers is never an easy task. The older we get, the more years we have in our present profession, and the higher our salary, the more difficult it is to shift into another field. However, once we have made the decision, we have to be prepared for hard work, perhaps years of reeducation and study, sacrifice in terms of money, time, and effort and many disappointments along the way to achieving this goal.

➤ Career counselors are valuable helpers in guiding us through the career-change process.

➤ Our first step is to analyze our background. First study fields that may be of interest to us. Once we have selected one or more occupations, identify those aspects of our background related or transferable to the new field.

➤ Don't overlook the intangibles that play so important a role in job success: drive, stability, intelligence, and perseverance.

➤ Career change may involve many months of retraining and financial sacrifice. We must weigh the advantages of a career change against the difficulties in accomplishing the change when making our choice.

➤ Resources we can use to obtain information about specific careers include reading trade journals in that field, studying websites of companies in that field, and talking to people currently engaged in the job or industry of interest to us.

> Sometimes the best method of changing careers is to start a business of our own. Perhaps we have a product or an idea that we wish to develop, or perhaps we just desire to be our own boss and operate an independent business.

> Business means investment. Carefully analyze what a new business requires in capital, working expenses, and reserves. Also consider that in most businesses we may have to forgo taking a salary for many months until it is underway. Business also involves risk. If we fail, we not only have lost our income for that period, but possibly our savings and that of our backers.

> On the other hand, the payoff of a new business can be substantial. Not only can we make a large amount of money, but we can accrue equity which builds up our estate. A good business can always be sold at a profit.

> Research the area we are planning to enter. Visit with prospective consumers or clients. Determine how well the market is currently being served. Get all the facts before making a decision.

Appendix A

....

ABOUT DALE CARNEGIE & ASSOCIATES, INC.:

Founded in 1912, Dale Carnegie Training has evolved from one man's belief in the power of self-improvement to a performance-based training company with offices worldwide. It focuses on giving people in business the opportunity to sharpen their skills and improve their performance in order to build positive, steady, and profitable results.

Dale Carnegie's original body of knowledge has been constantly updated, expanded and refined through nearly a century's worth of real-life business experiences. The 160 Dale Carnegie Franchisees around the world use their training and consulting services with companies of all sizes in all business segments to increase knowledge and performance. The result of this collective, global experience is an expanding reservoir of business acumen that our clients rely on to drive business results.

Headquartered in Hauppauge, New York, Dale Carnegie Training is represented in all 50 of the United States and over 75 countries. More than 2,700 instructors present Dale Carnegie Training programs in more than 25 languages. Dale Carnegie Training is dedicated to serving the business community worldwide. In fact, approximately 7 million people have completed Dale Carnegie Training.

Dale Carnegie Training emphasizes practical principles and processes by designing programs that offer people the knowledge, skills and practices they need to add value to the business. Connecting proven solutions with real-world challenges, Dale Carnegie Training is recognized internationally as the leader in bringing out the best in people.

Among the graduates of these programs are CEOs of major corporations, owners and managers of businesses of every size and every commercial and industrial activity, legislative and executive leaders of governments and countless individuals whose lives have been enriched by the experience.

In an ongoing global survey on customer satisfaction, 99 percent of Dale Carnegie Training graduates express satisfaction with the training they receive.

Appendix B

....

DALE CARNEGIE'S PRINCIPLES

Become a friendlier person

1. Don't criticize, condemn or complain.
2. Give honest, sincere appreciation.
3. Arouse in the other person an eager want.
4. Become genuinely interested in other people.
5. Smile.
6. Remember that a person's name is to that person the sweetest sound in any language.
7. Be a good listener. Encourage others to talk about themselves.
8. Talk in terms of the other person's interests.
9. Make the other person feel important—and do it sincerely.
10. To get the best of an argument—avoid it.

11. Show respect for the other person's opinion. Never tell a person he or she is wrong.

12. If you are wrong, admit it quickly, emphatically.

13. Begin in a friendly way.

14. Get the other person saying "yes" immediately.

15. Let the other person do a great deal of the talking.

16. Let the other person feel the idea is his or hers.

17. Try honestly to see things from the other person's point of view.

18. Be sympathetic with the other person's ideas and desires.

19. Appeal to the nobler motives.

20. Dramatize your ideas.

21. Throw down a challenge.

22. Begin with praise and honest appreciation.

23. Call attention to people's mistakes indirectly.

24. Talk about your own mistakes before criticizing the other person.

25. Ask questions instead of giving direct orders.

26. Let the other person save face.

27. Praise the slightest improvement and praise every improvement. Be "hearty in your approbation and lavish in your praise."

28. Give the other person a fine reputation to live up to.

29. Use encouragement. Make the fault seem easy to correct.

30. Make the other person happy about doing the thing you suggest.

Fundamental Principles for Overcoming Worry

1. Live in "day—tight compartments."
2. How to face trouble:
   Ask yourself, "What is the worst that can possibly happen?"
3. Prepare to accept the worst.
4. Try to improve on the worst.
5. Remind yourself of the exorbitant price you can pay for worry in terms of your health.

Basic Techniques in Analyzing Worry

1. Get all the facts.
2. Weigh all the facts—then come to a decision.
3. Once a decision is reached, act!
4. Write out and answer the following questions:
   - What is the problem?
   - What are the causes of the problem?
   - What are the possible solutions?
   - What is the best possible solution?
31. Break the worry habit before it breaks you
32. Keep busy.
33. Don't fuss about trifles.
34. Use the law of averages to outlaw your worries.
35. Cooperate with the inevitable.
36. Decide just how much anxiety a thing may be worth and refuse to give it more.

37. Don't worry about the past.

38. Cultivate a mental attitude that will bring you peace and happiness

39. Fill your mind with thoughts of peace, courage, health and hope.

40. Never try to get even with your enemies.

41. Expect ingratitude.

42. Count your blessings—not your troubles.

43. Do not imitate others.

44. Try to profit from your losses.

45. Create happiness for others.